*I dedicate my book to my parents, Jetty and Arlene Brown,
and to my lovely wife of twenty-nine years, Alma LeBon Brown.*

Moonshine and Living in the Deep South

By Cleveland Brown

The Scuppernong Press
Wake Forest, NC
www.scuppernongpress.com

Moonshine and Living in the Deep South

By Cleveland Brown

©2015 The Scuppernong Press

First Printing

The Scuppernong Press
PO Box 1724
Wake Forest, NC 27588
www.scuppernongpress.com

Cover and book design by Frank B. Powell, III

All rights reserved. Printed in the United States of America.

No part of this book may be reproduced or transmitted in any form or by any means, electronic or mechanical, including photocopying, recording, or by any information and storage and retrieval system, without written permission from the editor and/or publisher.

International Standard Book Number ISBN 978-1-942806-05-9

Library of Congress Control Number: 2015955505

Contents

Preface iii

Moonshine 1

Photos 41

Living in the Deep South 45

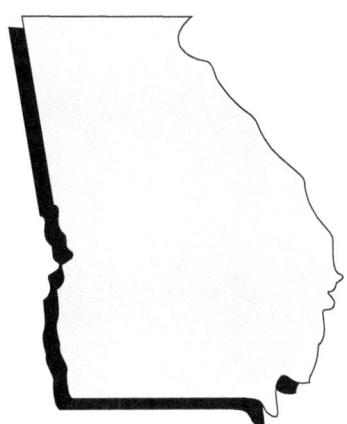

Preface

Ashburn, Georgia was born in 1888, the result of a new railroad line, the Georgia Southern & Florida Railway, which ran from Macon, Georgia to Palatka, Florida, intruding into its serene piney woods and open wiregrass patches. The citizens prospered for two decades from turpentine and sawmill operations. Following that, row crop farming took over the cut over woodlands. In the 1920s, farmers were into chickens, dairy, and larger cattle and hog operations that greatly exceeded the prosperity of the pioneer farms of the pre-1900 days.

In 1910, one of its citizens, J.S. Shingler, Turner County's first state senator and a large turpentine operator and land speculator, was declared the only millionaire in the Georgia legislature, according to the *Atlanta Georgian and News* dated July 19, 1911. After 24 years, the Betts Sawmill went broke in 1912, but as a place of employment, it had been replaced a year earlier by the Ashburn Oil Mill and the sawmill workers, many of whom were blacks which lived behind the sawmill, retained their employment by working at the oil mill.

In the 1940s, manufacturing began in Ashburn, particularly as it related to the manufacturing of pants for the war effort. By 1950, Turner County had a well-rounded economy of manufacturing and agricultural, but not everyone prospered. Few sharecroppers made enough to adequately care for their families and many turned to back woods moonshine production to make ends meet.

In February, 1955, one of the largest moonshine operations in the state, headquartered in Turner County, Georgia, was busted by Federal agents. The moonshine operation produced and delivered 15,000 gallons of moonshine weekly over an eight county area.

Jetty Brown, Cleveland's father, and his partners from Jacksonville, Florida, were small operators in comparison to this operation; however, the money they made from moonshine was significant.

This book is an inside look into that small operation through the eyes of a 12-year old boy and the role he played in its daily operations. For years, Turner Countians have seen pictures in their local paper of confiscated moonshine with the proud law enforcement officers standing nearby. Hopefully, this book will shed some light on the other side of those pictures.

The second part of this book is about Cleveland Brown's experiences as a black living in the deep South, more particularly, Ashburn, Georgia. Ashburn, Turner County, has consistently scored in the lower one-third as being among the poorest counties in Georgia.

Mr. Brown has a long list of beliefs about race relations in the South that the readers will want to consider.

You will quickly notice that there has been a minimum amount of editing of Mr. Brown's writing. Our intention is to present his writing as a true reflection of him. You will learn that rember means remember, thaire means there or their, theay or thay means they, and so on. It is common for the Mr. Brown to write in sentence fragments.

Our sincerest appreciation is given to Jeanie Marie Britt Edwards, originally from Ashburn, who served as typist. My role has been to help Mr. Brown accomplish his dream of getting his story into a paperback book.

Sincerely,

David M. Baldwin
Ashburn, Georgia

Moonshine

I have a story I would like to share with you all. A long time ago we lived about eight miles North of Ashburn to a small place called Sibley. On the Williams farm my dad was sharecropper farmer. One Saturday we was up in Arabi about three miles above Sibley and we met Johnny Haire. He had a brother who owned a farm in Arabi. So him and dad started talking and he ask dad did he know where he could get a good drank of moonshine. You see Johnny was from Florida. Dad told him yes. So he took him down to his brother-in-law because he sold moonshine.

So Johnnie took a drink and he said this is some good whiskey. Then he ask my dad had he ever made any whiskey. He told him that him and his uncle made some in the house on the fireplace. Theay had rig up a still and he ask my dad would he like to make some. Dad seen his boss and he gave them the okay. In about a week Johnnie went back to Florida. I was about 12 or 13 years old in 1949. A few days later we was sitting on the porch and we seen two pickup trucks turn in and come on up the lane. And dad said I wonder who.

Jetty Brown who is a black man and my father who was 6'5" or more weight 243 pounds. Smith who is white is real tall. He was about 6' 8", taller than my dad. He weight almost 300 pounds. Johnnie and Ralph who was also white was medium built. Theay was about the same size 5' 5" or 6' weight about 175 or 180 pounds. All three of them was from Jacksonville, Florida. Me, myself who wrote this book are black. I was born in Ashburn, Turner County, Georgia on November 2, 1937. All of this in this book happen in Turner County in Sibley, Georgia about eight miles north of Ashburn.

You know back in the day when my dad would tell me boy don't ever tell anyone anything that we do up here on this farm. I would not tell anyone. But you know back then moonshine was thousand dollar or even 2 million dollar operation. And even back then our state say, they was losing thousands of dollars in state and federal taxes. The bootleggers said if the state would have legalize moonshine and let them made it for the state's and federal government and payed them a fair price theay the state's and federal government would have not lost revenue. You see as bootleggers you had to do all of the work. You see anybody cannot operate and run a moonshine still because it is an art.

Anybody can't sit up a moonshine still. You see everybody don't know the ingredients. One thing that I was taught an early age is that what happens at home stays at home. I was young but my dad taught me that back then and today I am the same way today I might tell funny jokes. But you can bet Cleveland will not tell you what goes on at his house. I was raise like that. You cannot deal with anything illegal and run your mouth. That's what dad and those guys never got caught all those six or eight years theay ran moonshine because nobody ran their mouth. I loved to be around the moonshine still it was fun to me.

When I was about 7 years old in 1944 when I first knew that whiskey cus my mother an dad use to drink. They would go up to the county line Crisp and Turner County Line on 41 Hwy North. It was a beer saloon a white man ran my dad knew him. His name was Mr. Byron Parr and theay would go up thaire and buy beer. But he bootleg red whiskey. That was the first time I had seen any kind of whiskey I did not know what it was until I heard dad offer one of his friend some. He said man you want a drink. At first I thought it was kool aid. You know dad and l the blacks could not go in the front door theay had to go and go in a side door. Ad we use to go up to Arabi to my uncle's house he sold moonshine.

And that was the first time I had seen moonshine. I had never seen it was clear just like water. And that's when I started asking question about why it was not red like the other. He said because it is moonshine it be the same color as water. And I said dad why do you all drink that stuff. He replied because it makes you feel good. I said dad can I drank some he said no because you are too young. But I said I want to feel good like you and mom. So you know how kids are so when theay would carry me of with them I began to watch what theay were doing. One day my mother's father came over to the house and he pick me up and held me in his arm. I said pa-pa Mathis. Mom and dad has ben dranking that stuff that looks like water that make them feel good. And want give me none when I can feel good.

Boy, grandpa Mathis said Shorty, That's what he called mom but her name was Arlean, He said I told you and Jetty when you all was going out on Saturday night to party to brang my grand boy to me and your mother now he done seen you all drink that dam moonshine. What are you all trying to do? After that, theay did not take me with them grandpa would come and get me every weekend. I did not see them drank anymore until I was about 10 years old but my grandpa had passed away. He pass away when I was 7 years old. He has been gone a long time but I still love him.

I would sit down some time and ask my mother did theay still drank that stuff. She would say ask your dad. But she knew that was a no, no. I was not going to ask dad. I walk off and said to myself. She must think I'am crazy. I knew better than to ask my dad. So one day my uncle Charlie Fields and Aunt Lucy came over to visit. And I heard him ask my dad he want to sell some moonshine for him? Dad said I don't know. I will have to ask my wife. He said think about it. You see all of this was taking place on the William's farm eight miles north of Ashburn. In a little place you call Sibley. Where I became a teenager.

And I did not know later on dad would put up a moonshine still on the same place and run whiskey. I did not know I would get so deep involve with moonshine whiskey. But I did as little did I know a lot of things would happen before I would get to work at the still but a lot happen. First of all My dad started selling for my uncle and theay were making good money. You see my dad was a sharecropper and he did not make a lot of money just farming so he had to do what he had to. To take care of his family you see back then it was no welfare. Food stamps, Medicare or Medicaid for the Republicans to be talking about and people had to do whatever theay could to live.

And trust me theay did. But theay did not break in anyone's house because theay would shoot you back then and then call the law. But back then would make blackberry wine, grape wine, apple cider. I could go on and on but that's the way it was back then with us black people. And some white who were poor like we were. I can rember we had some whites live on the William Farm with us. Those that drank theay would come to the house and drank moonshine right along with all the black people that would be at our house.

Nobody got mad with anybody. You know why. Because my dad did not put up with that crap. I know because I was thaire. I can tell you this we had some white people that lived on the farm that did not drank. But theay were not like the whites of today. Theay would not have anything to do with our business. I wish I could say that about the whites of today.

Moonshine and Living in the Deep South — 5

You say theay try to be in all of your business. Back in them times, someone would come up missing.

Think my dad and two uncles were the only ones on the Williams farm that sold moonshine. It was one other man on the farm that sold home brew. And all kind of wine. But one thing about back in those days you did not hear anything about black on black crime. Then I know me and my dad use to go to a friend of my dads who was white. Dad bought moonshine from him. He lived in Crisp County. I can rember one time we went to his house one Sunday morning. And he told my dad. Jetty it is going to take a little while because I have to go across the pond to get it. So dad and I sit and waited. He put his boat in the water and began to paddle off but he was not gone long before he was back.

My dad told him that he was pretty smart to keep it across the pond away from the house. He said you know Brown we have to figure out a way to out smart the law man because if they catch us the only thing theay are going to do. My dad said what and he said give it to the guys that are selling for them. You see the law back then were smart. If you was not selling for them theay would catch you if theay could. A lot of times we would to town Ashburn on weekend's to shop the police and other law mens would know you are hauling and selling liquor down here and we are going to catch you. My dad would tell them that he farmed, he did not have no time to haul or sell whiskey by the time I get through plowing them mules I am to tird.

I can rember one 4th of July we had a dinner and dad and mother invited every one that lived on the farm. My two aunts hope her prepare the food. Dad had Bar-B-Qued a whole hog. And has cases of beer. I had to help mother and my aunts put the tables outside in the yard. By the time everybody got there we had all the food ready. I bet it was over a hundred people you never heard anything racist from none of the white people that lived there. You just could not here it.

Because back then the white people would say theay no better than us. And that's the way life was on the William's farm at Sibley. The people work togeather, party and drink moonshine and ate togeather, back then people respect one another but today theay don't. Why because the white man do not want to respect the black man that a black man is a man like he is theay will never get along. I seen dad take a gallon of moonshine and pour up a pint bottle without wasting one drop he had some study hands. I also seen him carrie two five gallon jugs of moonshine at one time. You now back in them days you had to be in pretty good shape because back then you might would have to run from the law because you never knew when you might get caught. So you had to stay ready. But my dad was lucky, he never got caught.

You know I was interduce to moonshine whiskey at an early age. I am glad I was because if I had not I would not know as much about it as I do. I would have not got the chance to see my dad and his two friends from Florida set up a moonshine still. And I would not get a chance to work at one. A lot of kids my age would have been glad to experience what I did. You know I often think about lucky I was to have a father like (Jetty Brown).

I know when a lot of people's read this book theay will say "wow" I wished I had a dad like Jetty Brown. He made the world go around. I learn a lot from him. For a man to have no more than a third grade education he was a genius. He count money in his head quicker than you could figure it with a pencil. I can rember him telling my mom one night he said Arlean you are my wife. You don't have to beg or borry nothing from no dam body. I take care of you and my son Cleveland. He told some of the people on the farm just as long as I crank that still up my family don't have to worry about anything. I do a little share cropper farming but that want take care of my family like theay need to be took care. One thing about my dad he put family first. I will never forget what he told me one night we were sitting in front of the fireplace in the living room. He said boy don't you ever tell anybody what we do up here on the farm you here.

You know at first I thought it was ok what dad and Smith and Ralph was doing until later on when my uncle Charles Field came running over to the house and told dad that the revenuers had find some moonshine to Grover's house his other brother n laws house. Later on I ask dad who those people will put your butt in jail. That when I found out it was against the law.

You know back in the late 40's an early 50's moonshining was the way of life back then. You know back then if nobody told the law about you selling or running whiskey you was okay. And if someone would go and tell the law you are selling or running moonshine theay then had to have proof of what theay told the law. When I became a teenager, dad and the guys was still running moonshine when I would get out of school do my chores around the house I would to the still and help with anything theay wanted me to do.

I would be one of the well-dressed boy in our class room. I got anything I wanted. You know my dad could have bought a new car every year if he had wanted to but he did not. He said when you start buying new stuff that you haven't been buying people began to watch you. He taught me that. He said if you have a million dollars don't change your life style. That's when you turn yourself up. You know when my dad was running whiskey him and Smith and Ralph I have been my dad with thousands of dollars back in the 50's.

I got a chance to talk to a person this year 2014 that my dad bought moonshine from her dad back then and we had a good conversation and she said she was glad to see me and I was glad to see her. You know when you are young and doing things like that you never expect to meet those people when you get grown. I did not but I guess time has a way of how it do things. I had never seen Smith or Ralph before until my uncle Charlies Fields brought Ralph to our house but after I got to know them theay were like family. Smith was the mean one. I don't think he was afraid of anything. My dad was about six feet tall and smith was taller than my dad he was a big white man.

On weekend's we did not run out Sunday's but we would clean up. You know back then the revenuers would use airplane's to try and spot your still from the air but most of the people down here in the deep south in Georgia, we had a lot of swampy places we could put stills and you could not see them from the air. Theay was more at risk to get spotted from the air than we was. I think that is why theay had to move their stills more than we did down here. But you know some time some of us would have to move but not much. I know a friend of ours on the river had to move his. He found out the revenuers had spotted it. And was going to bust it up. He got dad and the guys to come one Sunday night and help him to move it. It took them almost all night but theay moved it.

I can't help but talk about how much my dad trusted me at a young age. You know most kid's would have told their neighbor but I did not. You know why? Because I was raise up to not tell what went on at our house. That's what is wrong today. The wrong people know what go on in our houses. But not in mine. My mom an dad had train me. If anybody come and knock on the door do not open it let one of them do that. I never disobeyed what theay told me to do. I guss that's why dad and Smith an Ralph never got caught theay never got careless.

I was the lookout man. I done that and started the fire. But the part I like was the tasting the moonshine. I just want to say this I have heard people say moonshine whiskey will kill you. That's a lie. I know because I hope make it. If you make it by the recipe it will not hurt you. I drank it a long time and so did my parent and a million more people If people are running moonshine and using any kind of led pipes or car radiator, watch out.

Let me just set the records straight moon shine whiskey is made of what we eat corn. Rye or wheat. Sugar water. So if all of this kills people's what are we going to do. Anything will kill you if you eat or drink too much. So when someone come up to you and say moonshine whiskey will you. Can Cleveland Brown say so because I know? I have helped make hundreds of gallon. Now if you are sick and the doctor tells you to not drank strong dranks (whiskey) and you get a drank anyway rember he said no strong drinks. It could be red whiskey or gin white. Moonshine is not the only clear whiskey but theay but you know theay try and blame everything on moonshine.

But you know a lot of people in Ashburn did not now this about my dad Jetty Brown and me Cleveland Brown. You see if told you all it was a lot you all don't know about me and a lot you will never know. It will never be known because my daughter don't know if she did she would not tell anyone anyway. You know the parent of today don't teach thaire kids today like my parents taught me. Because the kids of today talk too much to the wrong people's. You see the point I am trying to make. Is if I had talk like the kids of today the law would have busted dad's Smith an Ralph.

Moonshine and Living in the Deep South

Before we made one run. When we are preparing for a run you have to let your corn work off. I think 3 or 4 weeks. If the weather is cool I think this is for North Georgia. But down in the deep south part of Georgia where I live it probley if is real hot like it be here about 8 or 10 days has to turn into a beer before you can run it I know some time you can get two runs of one bed. Now don't get me wrong you cannot get three runs. I all take that back. You can but the whiskey will be week and you cannot sell it. It is called low wine. We would just try to make one run.

One thing I learn about moonshine just before the whiskey come, the whiskey come it do what theay call puke. Drip drip, then a small stream and you on your way. Now all you have to do is fill your five gallon jugs up and watch the money roll in. But you be earn every dime because moonshining is hard work. And you run the risk of going to jail or even prison.

Most people don't know is if you ever have to move your still make sure you clean up. Don't leave things like sugar bag's or jar lid's but we were lucky enough we did not have to move but one time. Because the way we were set up. You see Mr. Williams did not allow hunting on his place either. You know like I said early. Pieces of copper and the other stuff shows that thaire has been some activity going on at that location. So, if you are planning on going into moonshine business these tips might come in hand for you. I know I will never need none of these tips because at my age I would not even think about it. Because my dad has passed I can do is tell the world my experience with how to make moonshine and watch my dad.

Smith an Ralph put it up that was something by itself to watch and to work around it was even more you know when I told my daughter about how my dad, her granddad had been in business making moonshine she could not believe what I was telling her. She said dad you have got to be joking I said no. She said wow! And she said dad did grandma. Know this? I said yes. She said grandma never told me about this. I said grandma never told anyone just like I did not until know.

I just like to talk about making moonshine it's an art everybody can't make it. I don't believe the people of today could make moonshine. First of all theay are too hard headed. Second theay talk too much and don't know who theay are talking to. To be a good moonshiner you have to not talk so much and not know anything. You see how long I keep this in me over fifty year's and if my dad was alive it would not be telling it today. See how long my dad keep a secret and do did I. What we need to learn is you don't have to tell Tom, Dick or Harry. You are a grown man so you don't have to.

I want to tell you something else you should know about this. In order to tell whether you have good strong moonshine or weak moonshine, you take a half pint in a bottle you shake it up an you will have what theay call bead's come up to the top of the whiskey. If theay come to the top and stay, you have one hundred percent moonshine. If theay burst time theay get to the top. You have week whiskey and it is not going to sell. If you ever have this problem you can easy fix it. If you don't have but a gallon or two you take one half pint of your week whiskey and pour in your strong moonshine. We had to do that when we first started off but we did not have that problem again. I know some time we slip but if you follow the recipe it is easy to follow and don't let nobody tell you put anything in it that not suppose to be in thaire. I would just like to see some good moonshine you can't found it any more. I would just like to have a half pint and shake it and watch it bead if it don't bead you have weak liquor.

A lot of people here you talking about running moonshine. Yes it is made out of corn that's right but we used <u>clean white corn</u> because dad said it made the clearest moonshine. I don't know about the yellow corn because we never use it. I guess you could use the yellow corn I don't know. I guss it would make beer their like the white corn. You have to run it all through a strainer I know we strained ours.

One thing about running moonshine you have to be clean with it. Make sure that the jars or whatever you put it in is clean. I seen some moonshine in jars that was not clean. You can tell when a jar is not clean it look's cloudy. Most people wash theair jars and let them drain over night to make sure all the water is out before theay fill them with that good stuff. The government knew that we moonshiners could make better moonshine on our home made stills than theay could on factory made still's because only us knew the art of making moonshine. All theay would had to do our government let us make the moonshine for them.

No theay want to make all the money and so that's why we had to go ahead and do what we had to do. Right today. You can't do anything unless the government wants a piece of the pie. Theay are the reason people break the law. Because theay want all of people's money

I would just like to see the lawmen try today to catch a moonshine still back in the day. It would be so funny. Because theay rely on thaire guns and do not use their brain you see back in the day. We outsmarted the law. But you see back then the law was not so quick with their guns theay used something the law of today don't have that's brain. Theay was just as smart as some of the bootleggers. That is why no one got serious shot or hurt when the revenuers would raid a still.

Most of the time when the fed's and revenuers caught one it was because someone had turn them up. Back then if you was making more money or selling to the wrong people you got caught or turned up. So you had to be careful not to sell to another moonshiner's costumer. You see back then if you had a big operation you could buy a sheriff. I know because my dad Smith Ralph bought quite a few in the days. Most lawman knew who had still's. Some of the peoples were their friends' and kin people. So nobody raised a lot of hell about a still unless (the Fed's) got involved then the Sheriff would have to do his job. Other than that we really did not have too much to worry about. Every now and then the Sheriff would hire a deputy that try to get smart but that did not last long because the Sheriff would soon get rid of him. He was not going to let one man cut his extra money off because back then theay hardly made anything.

I had clean the still up we had just made a run dad told Smith he was going to try something and Smith ask him what was it. He said I think I will double run five gallons. Smith said Jetty that stuff will be two hundred proof. Smith said man that stuff will take your breath. Sure nuf that stuff was strong. I did not sample it. So when dad ran those five gallons I had to clean the still again after he ran those five gallons you know back then theay say it took four men to run it but we ran ours with three men. It can be done all you have to do is do your part. To tell the truth I liked to do that again.

I started to ask a fellow one time about running some moonshine. Just to see would it get back to the law. You know how the people talk here all you have to do is talk about it and theay will take it and run. You can't hear much about moonshine around Ashburn now. I have not heard too much sense some certain people are no longer with us. But you know I ask a lawman a few years ago did theay every run up on any moonshine still's. His reply was no. We don't worry much about them anymore. But if we run up on one we will do away with it. Our main focus is drugs. I don't think theay will every stop drugs. Just like theay want every stop moonshine. Because the law had a hand in moonshine back then just like theay has a hand in drug's and everything else there.

It is 2014 and I just enjoy writing what I know about moonshine. I can rember one day I had put the coal under the furnace to start the heat where the beer could start cooking. So Smith had my little tin cup what I would have sampling the moonshine. He said Cleveland you need to wash your little cup. He was kidding me about it. Dad said boy that beer is going to start boiling after a while. So you need to get your stirrer ready where you can stir that beer. Where it won't stick to the side or bottom of the cooker. If it stick we will have scorched moonshine. And we don't want that. And that's bad for business.

One thing you have to do is watch your heat and you want have a problem with scorched whiskey. That is one of the reason we would run in the day time when you are wide awake and will not fall asleep and let the whiskey scorch and the other reason you can see better and watch out for the law. It's just better all the way round to run in daylight because most of the times the fed's will try and spot stills is in the day time because theay can't spot from the air at night. I know because all my life I have been around moonshine. I am not ashame to say so.

It's a lot of people in Ashburn GA that knew my dad Jetty Brown and my mother Arlean M. Brown. Theay have eather bought moonshine from him or eather sold him some. I know this is the truth. But I know it is true and theay do to if theay are still alive. But what the heck dead folks don't talk. If theay did theay would not tell on one another that is just the way theay were back then. I wish people were like that today.

I told you all I would give you the recipe for making moonshine. First thing you would have to have some firewood barrel's and theay proble are hard to found this day and age. You cannot take a chance on using metal or tin barrel because you could get led poison. Everything has to be clean the next step is the barrels have to be fifty to fifty five gallons filled the barrel about a foot from the top with water.

Then you put 2.5 lb. pounds of whole corn in the water let this sit about four days then you go back and add ten pounds of sugar to the corn and water. Ok now we are ready to put the cap on it. Ok we will take about five pounds of wheat or rye and put on the top of the corn. This is call a cap. Ok what we will do now is sit back and wait on it to work off. If we have warm weather it want take long about three days or if it's cool about five days. And while we are waiting we clean the still put the coal under the cooker we get everything In place. So when the stuff get ready we will be ready you may not believe it. It is a lot of work around a moonshine still. But once the still starts to run you ok. But you have to control the heat and not cook it too fast. I had a rake with an iron hand in it if it was trying to get to hot I would rake some of the coal from under the cooker and let it cook.

It's one thing about running moonshine you cannot be afread because when you afread you get careless and that's when you caught. Always keep your eyes an ears open. We would always know who we were doing business with if someone would ask dad, Smith or Ralph. About moonshine theay would check him out theay would have someone to check him out. If theay would found out if he had been in contact with the law. That was it theay would not have nothing to do with him. You know down here in the south back then if theay would put a black man in jail theay would tell them. If you tell me who all is selling liquor I will let you out of jail back thean theay called that turning someone up. But now days we have a new name for it. It is called snitching.

Back then if the right people caught you snitching you would not be seeing anymore. The people of today could not make it because theay talk too much theay have to man home boyfriend's and the men's today are not like we were first of all you can't tell them anything. So what you have today is a man's body with a child mine so what do you do. When my dad was moonshiner it was not for the white man. It was with the white man. But our black men of today theay doing. It for the white man and getting under paid and going to prison for them.

I know we had crime and murder's back then but nothing like today. Most of the times when someone killed a person it was about gambling or about a woman. But you did not have murders like we have here in Ashburn today. Back in the 50's an 60's when someone got murder here, the murder got caught and the law did not have today. But theay had better police officer's back then. The people at city hall back then was people and Ashburn. Not about money and power back then the people in charge cared about the people. Yes you heard the nigger word back then and you here it now. Back when I came up and the white people would help blacks. Those days want be back I enjoyed those days better back then than today. Simply because today I can see how where I grew up Changed and I don't like what I see law enforcements that don't seem to care about crime in Ashburn anymore.

In the 50's and 60's if you done a crime you got caught quick. But now here in Ashburn now. Theay try to blame the people in the neighborhood. When someone get in a fight or get killed theay say want nobody tell them anything. If it's at night in a neighborhood people's are in thair house. Theay are not sitting outside waiting on nobody to fight or get killed. And theay probley did not see anything. But the police we have today are quick to say the people are lieing and if theay don't know anything. It make them angry to be call a lie and theay are telling the truth.

First of all, it is not the citizen job to help the police do thaire job the citizen's tax money pay their salary the police suppose to be trained to do thair job and not the citizens. But maybe if our police officer would show the black neighborhoods some respect. If theay knew anything theay would help them. When older people like myself and the people in West Ashburn tell an officer we don't know anything. We don't and other words I am a grown man I don't have to lie to anyone.

I know those people in West Ashburn I lived over thaire with them over thaire over fifty years. If the older people tell you theay did not hear anything theay did not. I think it's a slap in the face for a police officer to call someone a lie. When he don't know whether that person is telling the truth or not. You know the police officers that Ashburn has today.

You see back then the mayor was over the police department — Mayor. Alex Story from 1954 -1972. He would have call every last one to his office and fired them and also the chief. First of all these unknown people from out of town would not be no police in Ashburn. And all of this kicking doors open and asking people where theay are going. A nobody going to jail for these unsolved murders in Ashburn. And a lot of more stuff going on in Ashburn. None of this stuff would not have happen in Ashburn. Or with the police dept. Under Mayor Story's watch.

I remember once what my dad told me he said you cannot sell moonshine and drank. If you will drink up the profit. I said well dad you use to drink and was trying to sell it. He said yes, but when we started to making it I quit because I needed to see which way the money and whiskey as going. When you in not only this kind of business you have to keep a level head at all times. Number one you are already breaking the law so you have to stay straight and keep your ears and eyes open at all times. And out of all you do sometimes you get caught.

Sometimes you will sell to a snitch and he will turn you in for a few dollars. And sometime it will be someone that you turn down who wanted credit. And you turn them down and theay turn you up. I know because one man came up to our house from town Ashburn. He had never bought any moonshine from dad. But dad knew him he wanted to get fifteen gallons and pay dad when he sell it. Man dad said hell no. Man you don't even do business with me. He said if you were doing business with me I would say yes.

But I can't I was sitting thaire listening the man told dad he would not have any good luck. Dad told him if he didn't get up and get out of his house he would not have good luck. Dad walk over and open the front door and they guy left dad told him to not come to his house anymore. They guy never came back.

But it never happen. The sheriff knew what was going on. But he was not about to go on the William's place without thair permission. Dad and Smith knew this so theay just kept on cooking that white lighting. I can remember theay left me at the still to go up to the house to meet someone who wanted to buy 100 gallons of moonshine. When theay came back I had ran almost five gallons of moonshine by myself. Dad look at Smith and said one day when we retire from this Cleveland can kept it going. Smith said jetty this boy still has a lot to learn but I am going to learn him. Dad said he has the nerve but I don't think he would take the chances we take Smith said Jetty you are right. Dad said Smith don't you think when we make this run we need to shut this thing down he said yes. And dad told me to start cleaning up that mean get up everything we would not even leave a grain of corn on the ground do away with all the sugar bags and everything.

Dad told Smith that he was going to hitch the mule's to the two horse wagon about dust dark. And me and Cleveland are going to load everything we ran today to our stash place because I don't want that much whiskey around the house. We would take it about a mile and half from the house. At our stash place, you could put about a hundred gallons thaire and have room left. We could run almost one hundred gallons from about noon until about an hour from dark. That was a day's work.

I know that some people here know more about whiskey than theay let on but theay make like moonshine whiskey is so bad. But you know and I know anything that we make and the government don't get anything out of is against the law. But instead of them talking with the people when theay caught them about making it for the state. You know Georgia has moonshine in the liquor stores. It's called moon over Georgia but it's nothing like what we made because when I drank I tryed some of it. Man it did not taste anything like ours. You know the state should had been charged for that bad whiskey. Theay don't know anything about making moonshine I could proble learn them something about moonshine whiskey.

Just like drugs theay are illegal. Unless the government is selling it. Just like my dad said theay will never stop people from selling moonshine. He said when the world come to an end thaire will be somebody standing around with a gallon of moonshine. I don't beleave we have any moonshine still's in Ashburn or Turner County. Because we have people today theay are greedy. Theay want to make all the money mostley white men. Theay want the black man down in South Georgia to do all the work take all chances and if caught do all the time. Back when dad and Ralph and Smith was moonshiner together white men were not like that I guess it was because theay were from Florida. Theay wanted dad to make just as much money as them. First of all most white men today a black man like me I would not trust one because he will double cross you and turn you in.

I love to think about I would be setting thaire looking at how red those coles had got. Man when theay turned red some moonshine was going to be run and it was. Back then the white man and black man stuck togeather. If anything went down theay was still togeather. Neither one would tell on the other. That was a bond theay had all the while dad and Ralph an Smith I never heard neather white man use the nigger word. I heard that word used after we moved to town.

You know later on I am going to give you a recipe on how to make some good moonshine dad and those guys could sure make it. It would be as clear you could not tell it was in the jug boy that stuff would make you high as a Georgia pine. People would say it drank so mile. You know anything you was drunk as whiskey. To show you how things change, I could be over at the store and say man I think I am going to sit me up a moonshine still. I went and ask Mr. (Joe Doe) if I could I sit it up down in the woods on his place. I bet you a hundred dollars the sheriff would know before I got sit up but you see we did not have them Uncle Tom's back then because we would have delt with it when we got thought with him he would not told anyone else. No we not killed him but he would have got one more but whipping he would had thought we was going to kill him, but no.

I know a lot of you guys came up in the 50's and 60's like I did drank moonshine like I did because it was cheap. You could get a 50 cents shot or a 75 cents shot or a $1.00 shot. We was able back then to get a cheap drunk. And after saying all of that. Behind every drunk is a hangover. How I well do I rember because I had a lot of them and I know alot of other people did too just like I did but I would not call any names. Why, because theay are still live today. Some are business men and some are not. But theay know who theay are you see back then that was all we were able to buy.

 Here is what I did for a hangover. If I was not going to drank anymore that Sunday trying to get ready for Monday I would drank me 1/3 cup of moonshine. Please don't drank any water. It will just make you drunk again. Drank lots of juice like tomato, grapefruit, lemon, do not drank orange juice because it is sweet it will make you throw up. But the recipe I gave you work's but I know for a fact moonshine hangover's is not as bad as those behind government whiskey. You know why because you don't have all of that chemical in it and everything I know because I dranked both kind's But guss what I know what is in moonshine nobody can tell me because I have help make I seen from the beginning to the outcome meaning from putting in the water, corn, sugar, wheat, or rye that's moonshine.

I use to drank moonshine, me and my buddies. We would mix it with grape fruit juice or tomato juice that will cut it and it want to be so strong. I had some friends white boys we use to drank with but those white boy could not handle that moonshine like we black boys. I would laugh at those white boys. Man theay would be drunk off a small glass full. Some of the those guys live today right here in Ashburn now theay are grown men and pass by me right now and want speak like I give a dam. Theay are no better than I am. We use to drank out of the same whiskey glass. Down in this part of the country in the deep south you can expect things to be the way theay are.

 But you know if I was a man that drank I would rather have me a good drink of moonshine. I never have cared about gin or the red whiskey. I would rather have moonshine then that red liquor. All those chemicals be in that red liquor that is what leave you with a hangover worst than moonshine. Moonshine that is made with corn, sugar, wheat, water, or rye. It is more healthy for you. If you just want to drank, it's nothing wrong with dranking as long as you drank the whiskey and don't let it drank you. You know it's a lot of people's don't want people to know theay drank. When I drank I did not care about people knowen I dranked. First of all, I was a grown man and could do what I wanted to do.

You know when I was dranking moonshine, I had a chance to drink with both black and white women. I found out that a black women could out drank a white woman and it took more liquor to make here drunk than it did a white woman. I never could figure it out and today still can't. But I know this when a white woman get drunk she will pass out but a black woman want. She will stagger around and want more that made me know that a black woman is more stronger than a white woman. But both woman's drank and have a good time. But I do not like to see them get drunk because when theay get like that theay cannot take care of themselves.

I don't drink but if I am out with a lady and she want one I will buy her a drank. You know just because I don't drink anymore, I don't have a problem with people dranking as long as theay drink the liquor and don't let it drank them. But you know what? If I drank today good moonshine would be my drink. I don't care what anybody say or what kind of liquor our government make at the end of the day good moonshine would be my drink. You know why? Because when I taste it, I know weather its good or bad because I had the chance to help make it. It's not many people that's still alive in Ashburn can say this. But I can that's why I am telling it.

I know while I am writing and telling the truth about our secret on the farm. In my early teens I had a chance to experience something a lot of teens did not get to do. I look at teens today. Theay don't have the brain to do what I did. Because theay are too hard headed. And theay think theay know everything. And don't know anything. I would just like to see a teen of today trying to do what I done. He would not even know how to light the coals and after he lite them he would not know the next step. When the moonshine star cooking and dad or Smith tell him its cooking to fast, cut the heat down he would not know what to do. Ok, I had a little rake what dad had made with an iron handle in it. In order to cut the heat all I would do was rake some of those fire red coal's from under the cooker and that would cool it down you know I once wrote for the newspaper here.

Some people's aid theay did not know I could do that. I told them it's a lot theay don't know about me and that's the truth. Jetty Brown is gone on home. He taught me well. I am so glad he did not leave a fool back here. Dad I think you know once you learn something you don't forget it you might not can do it. When you get older, but you can tell someone how. If theay will listen. That's our young people's problem today. Theay want take the time to lesten at what us older people tell them. That is why theay stay in trouble. Theay never learn one day theay will.

I am so glad to be able to tell about my growing up in Ashburn and Turner County. And to tell about what happen in Ashburn and Turner County and what I done as a teenager and to tell about my experience with the moonshine and how to sit up the still and the recipe on how to make. You cannot found a black teenager today as smart as I was and keep thaire mouth closed like I did. You just can't found one. You know a lot of men like me have been bragging about what theay dad did. But not me, I was taught better you know. I am sure a lot of people my dad, done business with after we move to Ashburn did not know what my dad done in the past. I know he did not tell them and I sure did not so this is the only time the story has been told. And one thing for sure I am the only one and the last one that know.

No one but me that's alive know this. So nobody can ask anybody about this because theay want know. So you can't tell me that we as black men cannot keep our mouth closed. White men can. We have had murders happen right here. In Ashburn black men murder by white men. The white people here know who done it, but will lie and cover it up and think we don't know it. But we do. But most of the time in a small town like Ashburn the white people wash them or give them money and that's the end. But I would just like to say all black people are not like that. I would just like to say most of us are just as smart as you are.

I would just like to share with you what my daughter had to say about me writeing this book. She said I did not know granddaddy did all of that. I said I know but he did. You see she was only seven years old when her granddaddy pass away. And she ask me how I knew. I said I was right thaire. She ask me what I was doing thaire and what I did and I told her and she said you all had got caught you would have gone to jail. Man she ask me all kind of questions about moonshine and the liquor still and how you make it. I told her to wait and read the book.

You know the more I write about moonshine, it comes back. Just like it was yesterday it all fall's back in place, but I think God that my mine is still good at my age. If you see some word's misspelled, I was almost sleep or tired so take it for love. Some time I had to stop and think back. Look I am in my 70s and I had to think back when I was 12 years old. I don't think we have many men's my age can think that far back and be right but you just cannot sit down and don't do anything with your brain.

Read books, do a lot of reading work puzzle's that's good for your brain. Rember if you don't use them, you will lose them. That's true I read every chance I get. I even go back and read old newspapers. I don't care just as long as I am reading. My daughter said I am the readest man she has ever seen. I said yes that's why I know so much because I read books and the newspaper. So always rember this you cannot ever read too much.

I just look how different it is here in 2013 and 2014. You know you don't here too much about moonshine no more. I guss because moonshiners like my dad and a lot of more bootleggers are gone. Come to think of it, it's been almost twenty years sense I even seen any. I am pretty sure they are still doing it in North Georgia. I would just like to have a gallon of good clear moonshine just to keep in memory of my dad Smith and Ralph.

A lot of people gave moonshine a bad name. But it was good for a cold. I know my mother would take some moonshine and mix with honey and give it to me and tell me to go to bed. That whiskey would sweat that cold out of you when you wrap up in your cover on the bed. The next morning that cold would be almost gone. You could nix it with lemon juice it was good for colds but boy it tasted bad. You see most everybody back then black and white dranked moonshine and had moonshine still's. Back then nabor's was nabor's and not pretender's theay was for real. If theay told you something you could depend on it. Not today. But one day things will change.

I knew that we ran a lot of moonshine in the South Georgia Tennessee and Alabama Florida but I did not know that Georgia ran more than our naboring states. But I did not know that we ran more moonshine than any country in the world. I research and found this out. So we are the King of Moonshine makers. And what we got for that. I would like to have some of those whiskey bottles theay had in the 1920's just for keepsake. I notice most all moonshiners lived on the farm. I would just love to walk through the woods and look. Especially in the fall of the year when all the leaves come off the trees.

I know some of the moonshiners would have to move thair stills because theay was not hide well enough. You know we never had to move ours but one time. That was because we found a better place to put it. And we hide it well. It could not be spotted from the air. And if you did not know where it was you would walk by it all day and would not see it. You have to keep around close where it looks thaire has been no activity nowhere close where the still is.

Back then the (Fed's) was smart. And you had to know how to outsmart them. Because back then if you seen a car park with nobody in it you could bet it was them walking the woods looking for liquor stills. So you had to be real careful. And out of all you being careful some people would get caught but we never did get caught. But dad say him and Smith had some close calls.

My Growing up in Ashburn and Turner County

I was sitting here thinking how I can rember when I was around six years old when my grand-pa Mathis would drive down to Ashburn and pick me up and take me back home with him. Theay lived on the William's farm up at Sibley. We lived at that time down in Ashburn my dad work for Bob Shingler. Theay had a small farm. Back thean my grandpa had an old Buick car. He cut it down and made a truck out of it. Back then the people would do that. Make Truck's out of cars. Theay would cut the body off right behind the front seats and close it back with wooden board's and thean make a wooden floor over the back tires and then build wooden side boodies and theay had a truck.

And can rember grandpa had a tairplace truck have any-one becise me heard of a truck like thait. I don't know it could had been a car and he made a truck out of it. But anyway I can remember it was a ugly truck. Back then black people could do and build anything theay wanted to theay did not ask the white man for two much. Theay would get out an do for themselves. That is what our young blacks are going to have to learn quick depending on somebody else and do for yourself that's the way our grandparents done. Theay did not depend on nobody. That's what my parent taught me and that's what I told my kid's do for yourself. Don't depend on anyone else.

I would like to see what it would be like know. In 2014 today with the moonshiners of yester year's it would be fun because the law men of today like to ride everywhere theay go. So theay would not catch any moonshine still's because theay are too sorry to walk. You see back in the day the (Fed's) had to do a lot of walking. If thay wanted to catch a still. You see theay tried it by air and still could not stop it. Yes theay blew up some stills. But that encurged the moonshine's to continue to sit up more still's somewhere else. But the law of today would have been lost. Because today theay go at thing's the wrong way. So what I see them do today I know theay would have made it. So what more can I say.

But I think the Lord to let me tell my story on how I was interduce to moonshine at an early age. You cannot and I don't beleave you can found anyone in this country that was interduce to moonshine at the age I was. I am very proud of how I was brought up. That's why I can tell the world and I am not ashame of it. And most of all I am not ashame of my parents. But I have never been ashame of parent's for anything theay done because theay did what had to do for us to survive. So I am glad that theay knowed what to do. I am not ashame to talk about moonshine because back then it was like a second job. For the poor black's and poor white's because all of them was share cropper's. Just like my dad theay work all the year and at the end theay would clear something like $700 or $1000 dollars for a year's work. So we had to go to moonshiner to make ends meet.

I was talking with some of the older guys like myself the other day and we were talking about old times and one said Cleve it ant any more good moonshine like it was long time ago. I said I don't think these young moonshiner's have a clue how to make moonshine. A lot of people don't know moonshine is an (art) anybody cannot make moonshine. You have to be raised in the country (woods) before you can learn the art of making moonshine. You have to be taught the arts of making (white lighting). City guys cannot make good moonshine theay just can't.

That is why our moonshine that's mad in the woods taste better than the government's moon over Georgia. You see I don't know how the government make thair moonshine but I know ours is better. But I know back then it was a lot of money in moonshine. If the government would had let people like we were made for them everybody would have money today. Nobody would be looking for handouts. But theay created thair own problem. I don't cater what nobody do or say (moonshine an drugs) are here to stay. Theay tried to stop moonshine as early in the 1920's and could not stop it. Theay tried to stop it in the late 1940's an 50's. That as a no no. And all the other year's was a no no.

You see it has slowed down but I know an you know it is still someone thair making moonshine. But you no don't nobody know for sure but the men's that's making it. So you see I want them to keep on cooking that white lighting and all you moonshiner's out thair with the real rescipe don't give it to our government because theay tried to put us in jail.

I have heard people talking about how long do it take to run a gallon of moonshine. I have never heard anybody talking about time. That has run moonshine are how long it takes to run one gallon or five gallons. The only thing we done was crank up at daylight and run to almost dust. Then we shut it down because you can't see and you don't want anybody slipping up on you. You would be stupid to run at night anyway because you would have to have light and that's a turn up right thair. But you know some people have tried it and got caught.

I know dad and Smith and Ralph would not even think about running at night. You know back then if the (Fed's) had a tip and proof that a moonshine still was at a certain place, theay would try and catch someone at the still. But if theay could not catch anyone thaire theay would go ahead and tare it up or blow it up. But back then theay would have wanted to catch the owner. But that did not happen fast. Because when you catch one the news gets around to the others. I am not saying what someone told me I seen this myself. I will tell anybody if you are a person that are doing something that is against the law don't tell anybody but yourself.

I was raised up to not tell what went on in our household. So I don't have a problem with not telling stuff. But in this same world today people will tell on thaire own brother. Theay have forgot about am I my brother's keeper. So don't depend on that. If you do you might just end up in jail or prison and that want be good.

I can't help but think about how Grandma Mathis would cook all that good food. I would eat when I would go over to her house. You see theay lived on the William Farm before we did. Grandpa Mathis had a cane mill theay would ground cane and make syrup. I use to go up thaire me and my mom when theay were making syrup and killing hogs. Mom would help grandma and my other aunt's cut up the meats and sausage. And theay would also make the lard. My uncle's would cut the cane down with long cane knifes. You know some time I just wish we could relive those time's but we can't.

I be telling my daughter about back then and she say dad, how can you rember all of that. I say well, when I start rembering some of the thigs the other just fall into place. Sometimes I will ask her how to spell a word. She will say "dad, you learned me how to spell. I said baby dad has been out of school almost a long time. She said I guss you are right. I can tell you if we had to go back in those days a lot of people of today would not make it. I am so glad I came along at that time. I learn a lot about how you can survive for your family and yourself. And that is what our young people of today need to learn because one day may just need to know how. I lesten at people talking today but guss what, if it come to my family surviving I know how

I have talked to some of my people in Florida and ask them do theay have moonshine down thaire. Some of them don't even know what moonshine is. I try to explane to them, but theay still don't know what I am talking about. So I just try to talk to some of my old dranking buddies. Most of them have quit drinking like myself. The only strong drink that I have is a sprit soda. But I love to talk about it. Some of the guys say, Cleve are you sure you don't drink now. I said why, theay say man much as you talk you sure you don't take a night cap. I said hell no.

But it smells just as good as ever. I just don't need it in my life. I tell anybody more to life than dranking moonshine. But don't get me wrong, I don't knock anybody that do what theay do with thair life. Because it's thaires. But you know I know a lot of guy's today that was out thaire drinking when I was. Guess what, theay are still out thaire dranking with I call baby's. Some of them are old enough to be those young guys granddaddy. But theay think theay got it going on shame on them. Theay are out thair drinking something or smokeing something. I just look at them and walk off. But you know I wish that all the older guys would quit drinking like I did. Then we could tell our young men's something about drinking and tell them where drinking will take them. If don't control it, and not let it control them.

You know I don't have any boy's I have two girls. I better change that. Two young ladies and I love both of them.

You know the rich has always said moonshine was a poor person's drink because its chepe. And that's all we need. But if we don't quit drink that stuff it is going to kill us. But anything will kill you if you drink or eat too much. You have to use common sense with anything. Yes alcohol any kind red or white will kill you if you abuse it. What I mean is drinking large amounts every day not eating. Just drinking yes first you become an alcoholic. And then it becomes a disease. You can prevent this when you are planning on going out having a few dranks make sure you have ate a meal before drinking.

That's where we make our mistakes. I don't care what you drink moonshine or red whiskey rember have a stopping point. I know some people that has never taken a drink in thair lives and theay ask me how did I get started and I told them the story. Not story, the truth and theay said wow moonshine whiskey is the best you can drank. But you have to have common sense about anything. If not you will pay the price and some time the stakes are high, but I still say today in 2014 if I drank today. It would be good moonshine because I would make it myself. Yes you can make moonshine today for home use and government will not bother you but you cannot sell it. Lesten good now I said you cannot sell it.

You see I don't want nobody going around saying I read in that book Cleve wrote we could make and sell moonshine and the government would not do anything to us. I know the government will get you today just like theay would yesteryear. So don't sit up a moonshine still in your front yard and think its ok. You will have some company and it want be customs eather. Always rember moonshine is still illegal in the State of Georgia. Back when we were doing it we had to be extra careful because the (Fed's) were real smart theay would walk the woods like hunters. Which theay were moonshine liquor still hunters and if you got careless theay would catch you. So you had to keep where you work clear I mean don't even leave a brick because theay knew what bricks was used for.

We were extra careful not to leave anything because we stored our supplies in our house and not around the still like some did you know I said early that you can make moonshine for your own use did I. But you know I would be willing to bet you if I got caught with one gallon of moonshine in my house today, I could not tell the law officer's I had that for myself to drank if I drank. Theay would put me in jail. That's the kind of law we have today. See theay don't know this. The only thing theay know is moonshine is illegal and you are not allowed to have any. So right thaire where I mention early our lawmen of today would have been lost back when we were moonshiners. But you know back then them (fed's and revenuers) were smart. Theay would in some parts of the state would go across rivers in boats if theay had been told a moonshine still was over thaire.

You know right today people still be asking about that (white lighting) call moonshine. I was looking the other day on computer at some still's one of my friends pull up for me. It brought back old memories. I just smile because I would if I could but my days are over for that. It's a new day and time for that because you have new people who don't have the knowledge or skills. Or how to keep thair mouth's closed.
That would be the problem today with running moonshine you see you cannot tell your friend's today. What you or doing theay will tell thair friends and the next thing you will know the law will be knocking on your door. So you see how different it is in today's time. You cannot tell everybody what you are doing. Please some time you cannot tell your brother because he may tell his friend's and theay may not be your friend and before you know it, you are caught. Just like that. So I truly hope everybody enjoy this book.

I know most older people like myself that know where I am coming from with this book about moonshine because those that did not drink had people that dranked moonshine black an white and some of thair parant most like own a moonshine still on thaire place's I know because I knowed the people and I know thaire children today that live in Ashburn like I do. But I am sure the children don't know the farm that thair parant left was bought with moonshine money

I know the very young it to 25 don't know where I am coming with this about working at a moonshine still. Or what it is but I am sure thair grandparent can tell them about it. It is an (art) to know how to set up a moonshine still and run it. Everybody cannot do that. It all sum's down to three words number #1 its an art. #2 knowledge #3 skill, so you see without anyone of the three you are lost.

So you see in today's time I do not think our young people could even past the test. Why, because theay are hard headed and want listen to anybody that is why theay could not run moonshine. If we had been like that we would have got caught. You have to lesten at what people tell you that's why dad and Smith an Ralph never got caught because when the people talk theay lesten even if theay was not talking to them theay still lesten. You know when you are running a business when people talk you lesten and running moonshine back then was a business to us. You know what. It was a good business. It made up for the slack the share cropper-ing left.

I am telling you if we could do it today you could make more money off moonshine than farming. I will do better than that you would make more money today off five gallons of moonshine than you would make off a ton of peanuts. So you see that' why our government was trying so hard to stop moonshine because theay was not getting out of it. And that is a no no with our government

I would like to see a moonshine still up and running 2013 but I know I can't unless some one I knew had one. And I don't but if I did nobody would know I but the owner and me. But you know and I wish we could just roll the time back and have the people we have today just to see what theay would do. I would like to tell anyone who is think about moonshin-er be sure to use all cooper pipe and please do not put whiskey in tin cans always use glass or plastic jugs. And don't use car radiators for anything in your operation for they contain led. And that is dangerous.

But I am sure that the moonshine still's today or modernized. But back when we ran I will say our still some people had to what we may say make thairs. But the one we had that came out of Florida was not home-made it was factory made all those copper pipes were shining like new penny's and the wooden barrels were new. But you know I bet you can-not found a wooden barrel around here anywhere. But you know all my grandparents knew what dad was doing. And theay would not even talk about it. And you know some of the rich white people here knew dad sold moonshine. It was some of them ran clothing store's right here in Ashburn. Theay would have him to bring them a gallon down to the store at Xmas time. Or theay would come up to the house in Sibley and get I theay would say theay rather have moonshine than red whiskey.

I told both of my two girls about drinking at an early age and theay lesten to me so far. I will always talk about moonshine because it's our way of making extra money back then. People that has never been poor do not understand what poor people go through. So moonshine was a life saver. A lot of people black and white made it because of moonshine. A lot of blacks then if it had not been for moonshine people would have lost thaire farm and could not survive. So you see moonshine is not bad as people say it is.

So you see any kind of alcohol is bad for you. If you abuse it. So you see we are sometime the cause of our sickness. You know you can sit a bottle of whiskey on a shelf. That bottle is going to move until somebody picks it up. So you see we cannot blame whiskey over something that we can control. I have been around moonshine all of my life. So if someone I know dranks moonshine I will tell them to make sure that theay eat something before taken a drink. You have to eat so that the alcohol have something to eate and not your stomach. When people drink and don't eate that's when theay get in trouble. But you know when I drinked I would always like to eate hot and spicey food. And I found out it would keep you from getting drunk. You are surpose to control the alcohol not it control you always rember that.

I can rember my job at the whiskey still was to start the fire. The way I would start it we had what we called wood splinters to start a fire. I could not use much of that just enough to start the coal. You know that's what we use to run the moonshine with because coal don't make smoke. But one thing back then the law could not just come on a man's place like theay do now.

But if theay could have theay proble would be in danger because my dad and Smith kept guns at the still when theay was running the moonshine and after theay got the still running my job was to watch the still and let them know when the whiskey began to come out. Because him and dad was watching to make sure nobody got close to the still. Smith had brought some guns from Jacksonville, Florida he had two 30-30 Winchester rifles and two Western Style pistols. And it would have been bad news if anyone lawman or anybody to try and slip up on those guys I knew both of those guys was not afreaid to shoot. Smith told my dad if we every have to kill one I know what to do with him. No one will ever found him but nobody ever got close to the still.

I knew what Smith was talking about and dad did to down the big dirt road where our mailbox sit. About two miles you cross an iron bridge about 100 foot was a road you turn to the right back thaire was a place call the going out hole. Water would be in thaire today and tomorrow the water would be gone. So that was Smith's plan. I know theay say a guy put in a bottle it show up somewhere else.

I am going to take you down memory lane one more time. We would clean our moonshine still right after we make two runs. The best thing we found out to clean and sanitize it with was hot water and alcohol that is all we used. We would take our worm, that's the copper pipe we use to run the moonshine through and run water through it to make sure it was clean. We let it about 3 or 4 hours to make sure we did not have any water in the whiskey. Most of the time when people get poison from the tuben theay use to run the whiskey. You cannot use lead tuben which is pipe some of us call it that's what has happen when you hear people say someone has died from drinking moonshine whiskey. Theay were using pipe with lead in it and the person that drank whiskey that was run through that pipe got lead poison.

A lot of people don't know theay think theay can use any kind of tuben but you cannot. I know because I was introduced to all of this at an early age in life. You see I had three good teachers, my dad, Jetty Brown and Smith and Ralph you see all three are one now I guss wherever theay went I am pretty sure theay met each other. I suppose theay are talking about all the moonshine theay made while theay was on earth. You know I might just meet dad and the guys when I leave this earth. I still say Jetty Brown taught me well. And I would not trade places with nobody.

I go along and think when we were moonshiner people did not try and get into your business like theay do now. You know back then blacks and whites go along better back then than theay do now. I guss it was because the white's would help black's back then you know my dad's boss could have easy said no. I don't want that whiskey. Still on my place. But he did not because he knew how much he was paying dad to work and that moonshine would take up the slack.

But the people of today could not have made it back then because theay talk too much and want to know your business some of the blacks an all the whites. You see the kid of today could have not keep this as long as I did without telling thair friend's but we knew better. Made money yes my dad made a lot of money selling moonshine. Yes, but he did not quit work he plowed a mule every day when we were not running whiskey.

Here is another thing he did not buy a new car. He could have bought two or three new cars. But he was not going to let everybody know what he was doing. You know it's a lot of people here where I grew up my dad have bought and sold moonshine to I should have said Turner County but theay proble don't know me cense I became a man but I know them. But guss I am not going to call no names what people don't understand about me Jetty Brown raised me up right. If he was alive I would not even putting this in a book. I will do better thean that. If my mother was alive I would not do it. But you know a lot of people tell me I am just like my dad. I am just short my dad was a big man. He stood about 6'7" and weigh about 245 or 260 boy he had some big hands. Boy if got his hands.

If I can rember correct I told that I could give the moonshine recipe. But if I did not here it is now. The ingredients as follows: #1 w#5 malt. Okay now we need a 55 gallon barrel. I would say a wooden barrel to be on the safe side. Now we add 25 pounds of white corn. Now we add the water but rember you have to add 10 pounds of sugar to each bushel of corn whole gran. Ok do not add sugar until the corn works off. If it's cool it will take it longer to work off. Make sure to not use too much water. Let the wheat be last. You put it on top of the corn. This is called a cap. Rember if it's hot it won't take long and you will have some beer. In the meantime cover the top of the barrel with some kind of net to keep birds, rats, and other things from getting into it. Okay now you have the recipe.

I am talking to the young men. How many of you out thair have the nurve enough to go and ask Mr. John can you sit up a moonshine still on his place. None Okay, now you all have my recipe on moonshine. But if you are anyone thinking about setting up a moonshine still in South Georgia don't tell anyone not even me. But always rember no one can turn you up but you. When you run or sell the first drop that's a turn up. But we blame somebody else. So now weather you want to or not I told you what we used. This same recipe. I don't know where you could get a still from today. But I am sure theay are still around. I would like to see one and make a pitch here of it. But I guss I will have to go somewhere else because I don't think we have any in Turner County. If we did it would be on news center 10 TV.

Getting Ready to Run, Let me Walk you through this first

We are getting ready to run some of that powerful stuff moonshine. First of all we have steam from the main water tank which goes into a third of a 50 gallon wooden barrel. Moves directly into a long thump rod. And into the bottom of a huge thump barrel which is filled with 190 gallons of fresh beer. At the beginning of the run, the barrel is a wooden hodges barrel with a 220 gallon capacity. From here the stream moves into a recharge or relay barrel of 50 fifty gallon capacity which can run "puke" then it goes into a dry barrel and from thaire into another into another thump barrel through another long thump rod. This next barrel holds fifty gallons of fresh beer. From there the steam moves in a large heater box which has the same function as those others I told you about the beer returning to be pre-heated through a valved line.

Some people's used (truck radiator no no) as the filtering or straining which is the repository for the final product. We never used radiator for thing in our operation because first of all radiators has led in them. You don't want no led poison anyone. I don't care how much you wash them out, nobody that cares about people would take that chance. We did not. Our still was clean.

I knew that we ran a lot of moonshine in the state of Georgia. But I did not know we ran more than anywhere in the world. So you can see how much money our government lost by not legalizing moonshiners to run the moonshine for them. Because we can make better moonshine than theay can. I know because have drank some of thaire (moon over Georgia). And it's nothing like the moonshine that we used to make. I know because I have hope make a lot of gallons an taste a lot of it. And I know that ours are better.

Most of us that ran moonshine lived on the farm anyway and we had hogs and cows. So the mash that was left after we ran the moonshine and clean up everything we would feed our mash to the hogs. It made good hog feed so you see we did not throw away anything. It would make some fat hogs and we had a lot of hogs. I don't know what the others done with thair waste unless theay bury it because when you get through with it you can't just pour it out in the woods because it smells just like whiskey. And you don't do that because you never know where the (fed's) are. Because back then if theay thought a still was in some woods theay would park thair cars or what theay was in and walk and lesten for noise. In the woods and try and sent to see could theay smell anything.

I know it is 2013 but I am going back to the late 40's, early 50's. My dad a white man in 49 in Arabi about 4 miles above Sibley where we lived on the William farm. The man het me had a brother lived in Arabi who Owned a farm thaire and he was up here form Jacksonville, Florida to visit him. My dad knew his brother so he asked my dad did he know where he could by a cool drink of moonshined. So my dad taken him to my uncle's house and he bought some and he took a drank. My dad say he said dam this is some good moonshine. He ask my dad did my uncle make it my dad told him no. So he ask my dad he know how and my dad told him one him and his uncle made some on a homemade liquor still his uncle rig up.

So he asked my dad he had a guy that would come up here and sit up the still. He ask Dad would he help to run the still. My dad told him to wait he had to ask his boss about sitting it up on his place. And he would get back with him. So he ask his boss and he gave him the ok. So about a week later man theay brought that thing to the house in broad daylight. I was 12 years old but I can still rember. Theay had another truck with sugar and corn on it and cases of five gallon Jimmy John Jugs I was sceared.

I had never seen that much sugar it was in fifty pound bags so theay unloaded the sugar and corn we had a big closet in the house where theay stored the sugar and corn. Theay let the still stayed on the other because theay had a cover on it so you could not tell what was on thaire.

So dad took Smith and theay look at the place what dad had picked. Smith said hell yes Jetty this is a dam good place those revenue's cannot see it from the air. You see back thean federal revenue's was bad on moonshine like theay are on drugs today. You see just like now anything the government isn't getting anything out of it is against the law. It was like that back thean.

So dad and Smith got everything set up. And theay was waiting for Johnny to tell them when to start. I will never forget dad's boss came over and met Johnny and Smith. He told to don't worry about the law because theay had better not come on his place unless he send for them. So you know back then that's the way it was. So dad started running the still thait Monday while Smith was coming up from Florida. I went down thaire with him to start the Cole's I put the Cole under the still while dad did what he had to do. So when Smith got thair everything was cooking so we just sit thair and waited for the whiskey to start coming out of the copper pipe. The pipe was ½ inch or ¾ inch.

It's been so long I can't rember. You know I ain't 12 years old any more. But I think for a man that is 77 I think I am doing good on writing this book. You can count the men in Ashburn on one hand that can do as well as I can. Man we sit thair and waited finely. It started to drop drip drop and then a small stream and next the stream is about half pipe then the pipe is full. dad and Smith was smileing when it started comeing out in a full stream. You would run 5 gallon about every hour. If you kept the heat to it Smith said Jetty boy the money is just about to start rolling in dad got (25) percent because we was keeping the sugar, corn and we had to stash the whiskey after it is made until theay get sales for it.

Me and dad would haule it off at night with a two horse wagon pull by two mules. We would sometimes haul it miles from the house. Dad and Smith had a route just like a mailman theay would do all of these Counties, Turner, Crisp, Worth, Tift. Theay would start on thair Monday and by Friday theay would be through. Every time we would make a run we would shut down and clean and wash everything before we make another run.

One thing about running liquor when you see the small stream get your jugs ready because it is getting ready to put out some whiskey. When the pipe get pull it is going to put out some liquor. It would put out 5 gallons every hour so my dad and Smith said that was good. Theay would run a ½ day if dad had to do some plowing. But if he did not theay would run all day but before the sun went down theay would shy down. Because theay would not run the still at night cause theay could not see who might be out thaire. Smith said he liked to be able see this sourrandings and you can't at night. Once you run the first batch and get a head thein you can start to deliver to your customers.

Moonshine and Living in the Deep South

Dad and Smith knew people in all the county's that surround Turner County. Theay had thaire route cut out. I don't know how Smith knew so many people up here and he was from Jacksonville, Florida. But he knew the law in every county.

Dad said theay was making a deliver in one county and the law pull up behind theim and turn on his red lights. Dad said he had never so scere in his life. Smith pull over and walk back to the lawman's car. And theay talked for a while and dad say Smith said Jetty bring one of those jugs and put his car. Dad said when got to the car, the man spoke to him and said I hope this is some good shine. If not I'm going to put both of ya'll in jail when ya'll come back through here.

Say he told It's some good shine because I have drank some of it. Man it as almost daylight when theay got back so Smith put dad out. He left to go and get him some sleep so dad layed down he slept till about one o'clock so he told me to go and start the coal under the still. I said dad today is Saturday and ya'll don't run on Saturday. Dad said son you are right. Then he said go out to the barn and put some corn down for the mules and hay. I said ok. I just fed the cows and hogs while I was feeding and want have come back out here.

Smith came back by the house and told dad he was going home this weekend to Florida. He told dad to hold everything down until he get back. So Smith went home for the weekend by our self so we cleaned everything up and got it ready for the next run. So the next Monday Smith came back and brought more corn and sugar that made us have enough to run a while. So theay did not start running till that Tuesday at noon. Theay had enough already made to take care of their customer.

So we all ate mother had fix dinner. Dad and Smith sat talking about money and stuff. Theay started off selling shine for $15.00 for five gallon and raise it to $25.00 per five gallon. This was 1950. These guys were making a lot of money. I know because my dad was making a lot of money too because I had anything I wanted was riding the school business to Eureka High School. I was one of the wellest dressed guys in school. The rest of the kids in school would be askin me where I bought my clothes from. I told them mother bought them. I don't know where she bought them from. Theay would say theay sure is pretty and I would say think you.

If it had not been for moonshine we would have had a hard time. Because back then theay had something theay call a run bill. Theay would pay you so much money a month on the farm. My dad would get $15.00 per month for him and me and mother. So my dad had to do something on the side also. Mr. William had two chicken houses and he would pay dad and mother to see about the chicken on weekends. Theay had to feed and water them, but he paid them good $15.00 each on weekends. Back thein $15.00 was a lot of money. But people had to look out for themselves. So when Johnny made dad a deal he took him up on it. So moonshine was no bad deal unless you got caught.

Dad and Smith never got caught you see. Johnny was the money men. He never even went down to the still. I can rember one day we was on the front porch and look down the lane what came up to the end and seen the sheriff car parked on the big dirt road. See it was the people that came up from Ashburn and bought liquor from dad by the gallon and theay thought theay would catch someone coming from thair with some liquor. But what they did not know was that Jetty Brown was a smart man. While theay was sitting waiting for them to come out thaire way we had a back way theay could go out right by the bosses house. And be back in Ashburn selling liquor. And theay are still up thaire waiting on them to come down the lane out of the gate where theay can catch them.

I can rember one Sunday morning my dad woke me up. He said get up we have to go to the mister S and pick up 20 gallons of moonshine from the boy's coming up here from Ashburn. We done sold all we had made. We want run anymore until Monday. I said ok dad I am getting up. So dad went on the door to crank up the car. So I ran out to get in the car. So we headed to Crisp County. Okay when we get's to Arabi which is about three or five miles from Sibley where we lived. He made a right hand turn just as we passed McKinze's drug store back then. And we went across the railroad tracks and we went way back in the woods. I said dad how far more we have to go. He said not far. He said that's the house yonder. That white house with the pond behind it. So dad pull in the yard.

A white man came out of the house smoking a pipe. He said Jetty what you doeing up so early. He said mister S, I need to borrow 20 gallons from you until we crank up Monday. Some guys are comeing up from Ashburn. It's four of them and each one of them want five gallons. He said ok Jetty. I got to take my boat and go across the pond and get it. It want take me long.

Sure enough it did not take him long to get it. So him and dad put it in the car. He said what you doing up so early. I said to ride with dad to your house. Dad was telling him how much I helped them at the still. He said that's right Jetty learn him while he is young. So dad said Mister S, I got to run where I can be at the house when those guys get thaire. Sure enough when we got back those guys were thaire waiting on that moonshine.

You know it was a lot of money made in moonshine back then. And you know what? A lot of Sheriffs and police chief's was bought back then. I use to here Smith tell my dad. Jetty you need not worry about those SOB's because theay have been bought and paid for. And theay damn better not double cross us. If theay do it will be hell to play. Smith said thay had bought the sheriffs of Worth, Crisp, and Ben Hill counties but not Turner. One time my dad and I went to town and Turner County Sheriff Wesley Fiveash says to dad, "Jetty, I know you boys making moonshine up in the woods." "I just want you to know, I'm going to catch you." My dad replied, "Sheriff I plow behind a mule all day and the last thing I want to do is run moonshine all night." But that was just it, we run our moonshine during the day when we could see if anyone is coming, and we made our deliveries like a newspaper route at nights.

And do you know what? I never seen any white men any nicer than those three men from Jacksonville, that my dad worked with. You just don't see it anymore, but I guss it was because theay was from Florida. Theay would give me money and when theay would go home, theay would bring all of us something when theay would come back. You know that's been a long time. But when I start writing about it, It seem like yesterday. Those days are gone.

You know back in the day when my dad would tell me, boy don't ever tell anyone anything that we do up here on this farm. I would not tell anyone. But you know back then, moonshine was thousand dollar or even a million dollar operation. And even back then our state say theay was loosing thousands of dollars in state and federal taxes. The bootleggers said if the state would have legalize moonshine and let them made it for the state's and federal government and payed them a fair price, theay the state's and federal government would have not lost revenue.

You see as bootleggers you had to do all of the work. You see anybody cannot operate and run a moonshine still because it is an art. Anybody can't sit up a moonshine still. You see everybody don't know the ingredients.

One thing that I was taught at an early age is that what happens at home, stays at home. I was young but my dad taught me that back then and today I am the same way. Today I might tell funnie jokes. But you can bet Cleveland will not tell you what goes on at his house. I was raised like that. You cannot deal with anything Illegal and run your mouth. That's why dad and those guys never got caught all those six or eight years theay ran moonshine because nobody ran thair mouth. I loved to be around the moonshine still. It was fun to me.

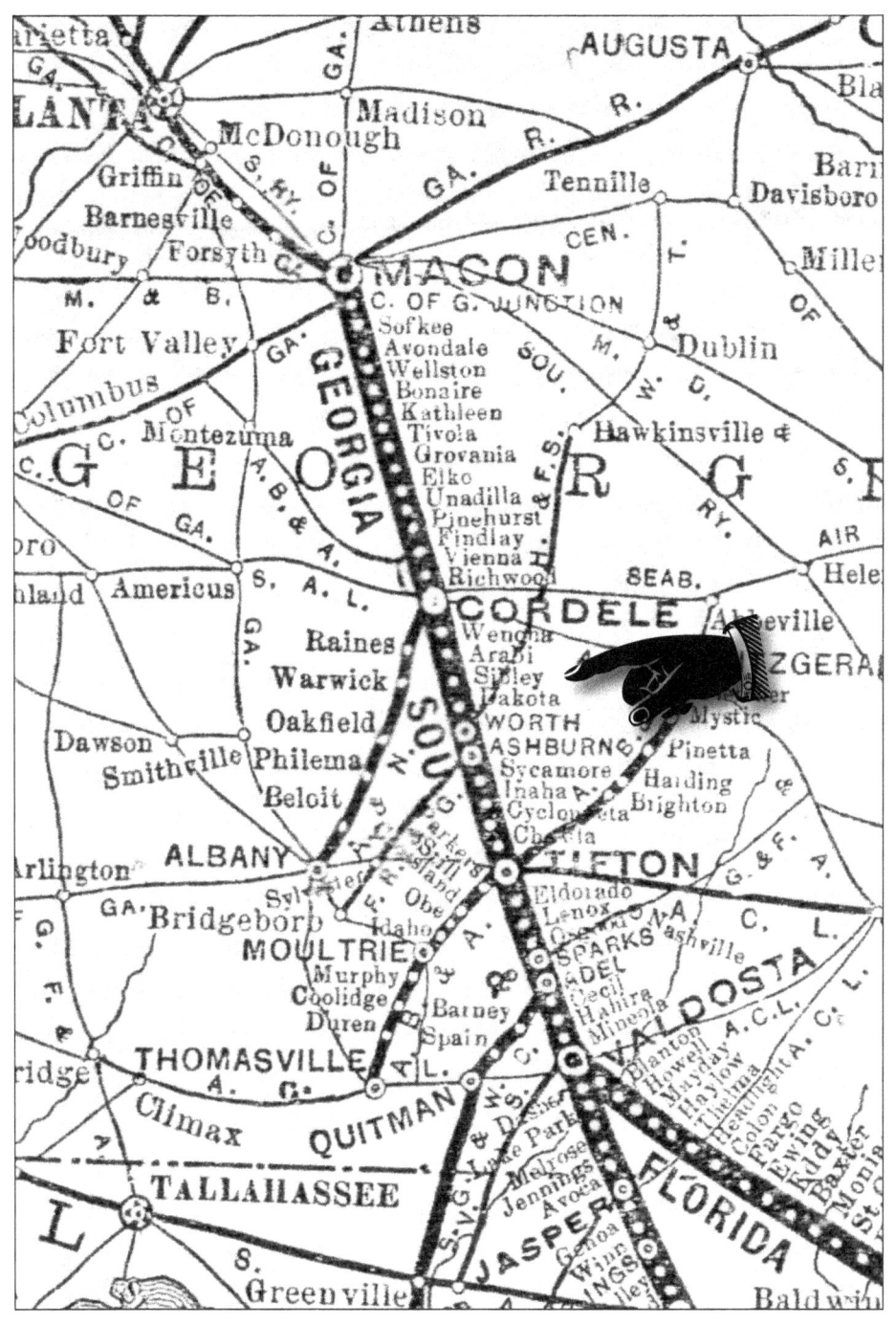

1913 Map of G S & F Railway showing location for Sibley, Georgia.

Mr. Brown attended first grade in 1943 at the New Hope Baptist Church in Sibley, Georgia.

Mr. Brown examines moonshine still at the Crime and Punishment Museum, Ashburn, Georgia.

Moonshine and Living in the Deep South

Living in the Deep South

Growing up in Ashburn and Turner County, I was born November 2, 1937. My parents were Mr. J.B. Brown and Mrs. A.M. Brown. I was born north of town on Warwick Hwy. The house I was born in had only two rooms, a kitchen and bedroom. We had no inside bathroom, no running water, no electric lights, wood stove. My parent said we lived with my grandmother until she, my mother, was able to go home. My dad told me at that time. Was working for Mr. Herman McCard at the Standard Oil plant. Witch as located where Genaz Store is on my M.L.K. I think he said we were living behind The House by the Road.

He was living in Mr. Bob Shingler's house. You know back thean if you live in a man's house, he wanted you to work for him. So dad went to work for him and work for him a long time. By this time, Mrs. Shingler wanted my mother to cook for her at the house by the road. I was not old enough to go to school. So I went with mother to work. Boy I will never forget the good food I ate at that house.

We moved about 8 miles north to a place theay call Sibley. This was in the forties. My dad was share cropper. We stayed up thaire until I was about 14 years old. Then dad decited he wanted to move back to town. That's when we moved to the housing project on Stevens Street. Boy, Ashburn was on the ball.

I was going to Eureka School that was in 1952 we would have a lot of fun in school. But we had to get our lesson because Mr. Dye, Mr. King did not want anything but A's so brother if you did not want to get your pants smoked, you better get that lesson.

Now let's get back to Ashburn back then my town. People you might not beleave me but every building you see down town was open. Man I been wanted to write about my town Ashburn but did not have the time. But now, I am retired and I can. So brother I'm going write about it while I can still remember it. I will not lie about anything I will tell it like I saw it.

Me and my uncle cusin we was the 3 ace's when you seen I Kep looking it's two more and you did not want to cross us we would clean the street with you. Forget about that, let's get back to my town Ashburn. Boy I remember when I could go to the movie for 9 cents that's wright we had a movie here in Ashburn sure did but for some strange reason it burned down. But we talk about that just yet. But I know it is somebody out thaire just as old as I am know why and how it burned down.

That I will never be seen in this life time again. Down below Smith as Jinkins Insun Real state. On the corner was my ladies shop run by

Mrs. Perlee. We will keep going cross the street was the bus station and drug store by Dr. North. Ellis Farm and Equipment Service Station and Standard Station. Ha let's go up US 41 Hwy. Let's start at the Methodist Church. All those houses from the church down were Shingler's and McKenzie's. And my grandmother cook for all of them. And help raise all thaire children.

As a 14 year old boy in Ashburn it was hard. Because you did not have good school books you had to use book's that had been mark all in pages torn out. It was hard. This was in the fifty's we had to walk to school we did not get free lunch. We had to take our lunch from home but we made it. Our basketball court was hard clay but we won games.

Poor people had a hard time back then and are having a hard time now. But God bless Mr. King along with Mr. Dye we made Eureka. Most people here us talking about Eureka and don't know we students hope build Eureka. The army gave us those army old barrack and Mr. King and all of us put them togeather. So that is Eureka is so dear to our harts. That is why one of the students made this statement you can tare down the building but you can't our hart's.

I seen a lot of black school's torn down in Southwest Georgia. Some of the school just need a little repair. But I will never forget the good old days growing up in Ashburn. We had a lot of stores in town open.

But I herd my great grandmother say one time that Ashburn had a curse on it. But I did not know what she said it as talking about She said a man was hung in the old jail. She said some bad things had happing in this small place. She also said nothing good would come of it And she told my grandmother she might not live to see it but Ashburn would dry up and go down and look like it is 5 years ago. Ashburn was ok to live in you had a lot of people and you could get a job anywhere. People would drive up and say you want a job and we would say what are you paying theay tell you and if you like thaire price ok if not theay would drive off. Theay would not say theay want work. Theay would say that is all I can pay now.

We have work in watermelon back in the 60's and early 70's for 15 to 20 dollars a day. If we got what the man wanted by 12 o'clock we still got payed for a day's work now if you make one hour overtime you have to go to work the next day one hour late. It took me a while to found out about my little home Ashburn what few jobs here the one's that ride around in new trucks. Supposed to be bosses make big money don't know anything and rideing the working man's coat while he being under payed.

You know things have not changed much sence I grew up. But I notice thaire is not job's to support a family so what do you do most people move. We have lost alot of our people to Tifton. So what is the problem we cannot get jobs to come here will some body tell me why. I rember my dad told me he said son if it's your home town and it can't support you, move. So Ashburn you are going down. Your people are leaving you.

I left Ashburn in the 60's. Lived in Calhoun, Georgia about 90 miles above Atlanta for about 2 ½ years. My dad and mother kept begging me to come back. That was the biggest mistake I ever made in my life. I don't know what it will take to review Ashburn. I hate to see the town go down. What about those old buildings why don't the owners of them give somebody 1 or 2 years rent free to fix them up and use them in that way. The owner would be getting fix up. Ok, after 2 year should be made enough munee to pay for fixing the building. Ok, now we start paying rent. In that way we might be able to save some of Ashburn if not all of it.

I would like to see a movie theater a show shop also some more grocery stores how about a meat house. When I was growing up in Ashburn West Washington was nothing but a dirt road Gold peanut was Ashburn Peanut Co. and before it was Ashburn peanut theay called it Ashburn Oil Mill because my father work thaire at that time. WE also had a cotton gin in Ashburn we had saw mills we had Cordele Concrete Folsom Construction Co.

In the 60's 70's some in the 80's but after that job's begain to shut down. Jobs would come here but would not stay long so I begin to ask people why job's come here and stay a little while and leave. I don't know why jobs would come and leave, come and went after Coat's and Clark but I talk to the plant manager, we were eating breakfast and he told me why theay left because Ashburn would not give them tax breake. That is why theay left. Ok we had mobile home plants. Theay closed down Ashburn Hardware shut down. We don't have anything here people are leaving something is wrong. Is the curse working on Ashburn?

We need leadership or do people need to come together and see what we can do. Thaire is no stores on North 41 nothing but buildings with nice fronts out backs the whole town is falling apart. If we people don't do something in 4 or 5 more years, the whole town will be on the ground.

I don't know look like the older people like myself don't care a lot of them grew up here just like I did but I guss theay done gave up. Ashburn once had county and city over 12,000 people. We need to get togeather and found a way to get some of the store's open. But let's get back to the cotton gin as located on the corner of S. Gordon E Washington. Ok Farmer's Furniture Co., Piggly wiggly parking lot is on the spot where the gin was not the Rogers Plaza.

When you exit Piggly Wiggly's parking lot north back to Washington make right turn was a small café call The Rib Shack. We would play music and dance. Down below the café were Bancroft Wig shop and Pylant Insurance and Keith-A-Que was a big tamato Plant shed where theay packed tamato plants. Over where Fred's and Dollar General was the Black Methodist Church. Ok, we cross over to the other side of the Washington Street and go back west.

On that side of the road thaire was 3 or 4 gunshot houses and one big house. I think it was right about where City Hall is now and above thaire it was two beer saloon's one was run by King Solomon Burk's, the other dad's was a clothing store call Dunn's Ready to Ware everybody traded with Mr. Dunn. Because you could get clothe and pay by the week. You could pay four dollars a week.

The next place was a pool hall and barbershop. Mr. Willie Burke ran the pool hall and Mr. C.Q. Leary ran the barbershop. Mr. Burke also had a café in the old Napa building where Bush furniture store is now.

Over in the housing project on Steven's Street where I grew up, it was a lot of familey's lived thaire it was as follows. The Westbrook family, the Hall family, the Burk family, the Field's, the Brinch family, the Mathis family, the Kimbles, the Martin, the Jones. Also the Elliotts, the Lewis, the Moore's, the Brown's, the Shine's. It is a lot more of my friend's lived thaier we had a lot of fun.

We did not know what drug's was after school we had a basketball goal on the back of the project. So we would go back thaire until dark. Then we would go to the house and get our lesson for the next day. We had a little café before you get to the project call the White Ace. We would meet down thaire on the week end's play the juke box and dance and play with the girl's. You could not here anything about drug's in the black naborhood. Black's back then did not do drugs. Theay would Drink beer and whiskey on the weekend. But would be ready to go to work on Monday.

Me and my cusin and my mother's baby brother, we would run togeather. Boy if you did not want to get beat up you better not mess around with either one of us because we did not play the radio.

We would love to go to Mr. W.C. Britt's grocery up on Jefferson. But Sam Gamble's wife owned the house and the old store. I rember a big fair came to town. It was in the ball park by the recurse center. It was so big it had two farris wheel and it reach almost to tomb's Street that was the biggest fair I think that ever been here.

On the West Side was more cleaner back then thain it is now. But it was fun back then. Everybody got along. People was not violent back thein if anybody got killed back theian it was very unlikely. People back theian respect one another. And theay got along with each other. Myself and my cusin and other guys we would box and lift weight's. We did not have the money back then to buy them so we made ours. Ok we got two 5 gallon bucket's a long piece of pipe ok we will each bucket with wet cement bucket on each end and we have our bar bell weights. You might not believe me but those things weight 200 pounds. But some could press those things.

Myself I always was small you might say when I was around 16 or 18 years old. My weight was around 140 pounds. But we work with weights that change.

It's a lot of stuff happen in Ashburn has never been told about the black lady that my grandmother told us was killed by three white men because she would not dance for them nude. Theay the people were giving a party that night and had her to wait on the tables. Those guys started dranking and that is what happened. The house still stands today on south Main Street with Brick's all around. I ask dad about it. He said yes Cleve it is true. He said and the sad thing about the whole thing is theay got a black man to take the body and hide it in the woods on his little farm off Sugar Hill Road. Her body was found month's later by a man working turpentine in the woods. My dad said the day the worker found the body it came up a bad cloud and pour down rain and the weather was real bad.

I can remember the police station was at the intersection of Main and Washington. On Saturday mother and dad would go to town and when theay would come back mother would say we went by Mr. Wisham Fish Market. We are going to have fish for super and your dad is going to make the ice tea.

We have had some hard times. Black people at one time was not allowed to park on the front street. Theay called it back then. But it is Main street today and I remember my dad telling my mother theay took a black man's car.

The next day my dad and Uncle Tom went down town to get something from the store and theay said theay heard some white men talking theay said that nigger don't need a new car. My dad knew the man from Florida who's name was Guncie. The man was so scared the people where he bought the car from had to make a trip up here and get the car for the man.

When I grew up was real racist back then. And it is 2013 and it is not much better but change is going to come. I might not live to see it, but my two girls and grand boy's will I hope my girl's Amber and Michelle theay are my heart. Maybe one day theay will read this book that dad wrote. So much for that.

Let me get back to where I grew up. I will always be grateful to Eureka High School. It made a man out of me. I also want to thank Coach Dye. He was my track coach, what a man. He played a big role in my life. I will never forget him. He was training me in track to brake Jessie Owens Track Record and I could had easy did it. Because I was fast, but somewhere girls got in the way. And so well you know the rest but through it all I had fun going to Eureka School it will always be with me.

I am going to dedicate this book to my wife who passed away November 22, 1997 and my Mother who passed away April 3, 2011, my father who passed away January 27, 1994 and my two daughters Ambery and Mechelle.

Ok, we will travel down south gorn down to Yo Ho Apartments. Kennedy's Turpentine quarters begain all the way to Adam Street. All of John Dye Lane, all of Freddie Weston lane. It was probably over 100 house jam in thaire. He work a lot of men this was in the 50's.

Scott & Hearn Lumber Co. Theay work a lot of men that was in the 50's also. It was located where wood component across the rail Road in front of Turner County Stockyard. My dad and uncle work at the sawmill was located down 41 Hwy. My father and uncle worked for many years.

I tried to get in the Navy at 16 but my mother would not sign for me so I stayed in school. So after school I work around town but I finally got a job with a contractor working on I-75 Hwy. We work from Tift County on up so one day he ask us guy's did we want to go with him to Atlanta. It was three of us. Myself, Curtis and Fat. So the other two guys said yes. But I had to think about it because I had never been off from home. It took me a couple of days and I said I would go. So the next Sunday we left we got up thaire. It was ok. After I was up thaire for a while so I was coming home every week.

I had never been away from home and Ashburn so it was hard for a while until I got used to it. Then I would come home every two weeks then once a month and finally I would not come home at all. I would mail money home after I learned the neighborhood. I would come home once a month. I liked the place it is about 90 miles above Atlanta. The name of the town is Calhoun, Georgia. Theay have a ton of carpet mills thaire. It is what you might call textile town. You have Mohawk and Queen's Carpet Mills and a lot more. Man it as a booming town in then, so I know it is booming now.

I met a girl up thaire by the name of Pat. She had just started teaching school and boy she was pretty. So we started dating. I probably would had marryed her if I would have stayed up thaire. See I was doing Construction work on Interstate 75 and it begain to rain and when it started to rain in North Georgia, it rain's weeks at the time. So we had to come home that is where I made my mistake was coming back to where I grew up. I should have stayed up thaire and got me a job to one of those carpet mills. But that is water over the road. I am back in Ashburn. But things were ok until about the middle 70's when job's started shutting down.

Job's started to leave, Store's began to close, and more job's began to lay off people. And more stores began to close by the 80's. We had lost a lot business in Ashburn in the late 80's or early 90's. Coats and Clarks, One of Ashburn largest job's left town. I did not know why theay left until years later. I was told that the City would not give them a tax brake. I don't know what the city told the people. Mobile Home Factory left. Ashburn began to go down like a flat tire and been going down ever since.

We live in a town that have had a lot of bad things happened. When you live in a place with no job's, no recreation for the young people, no bowling alley, no swimming pool. When young people have too much free time, that's when theay get in trouble. And the next thing is crime. All of this could have been avoided if theay would have had something to do beside walking in the street. Long time ago it was a swimming pool skating rink in West Ashburn but when all the school's and everything had to mix the white people said the Shriners Club owned the pool and the skating rink so you know the rest. Theay claim the pool was not safe to swim in. But you know it was safe before so what happen. Nothing was wrong with none of it. Something was wrong with the people it was back in the 60's and you and I know what it was.

Ashburn is not getting any better. I would advise the black kids that is getting out of school to leave because it is nothing here for them. Got to Atlanta or Florida if you hang around you not going anywhere but to fail or prison because you are already labor that you need to go where people don't look at the color of your skin theay look at what you can do. You got a good education so don't waste it you got it in your head nobody can take it away from you.

I talk to my daughters every day to get out of here as soon as she can don't get stuck here like I did. Thaire is nothing here for young black people. I talk to people every day about jobs here. Theay give me the same old story we don't have a work force or people won't work. People will work if you pay them a fair price. You can't expect a heavy equipment operator to work for $10.00 per hour or a truck driver to work for $7.25. It's not going to happen.

Worst now than when I was growing up. Number 1 you have too many police for a city of little over 4,000 people You don't need that many. When I was growing up we had about 9,000 people or more. I remember we had 4 police, 2 on at night, 2 on day time and theay would walk the street and shake every store door to make sure theay were locked.

Now you have policeman park under shade trees, sleep or out to Shoney's setting down drinking coffee. Rode around doing nothing at the end of the day. Theay drive the police car home. That is wasting tax payer's money you are paying the officer to work he should have his own ride to work. The chief should be the only officer to drive his car home. I don't know where theay get them from but theay are not friendly. I seen the lady police theay are rude. I seen theam work a wreck

Theay don't know how to talk to black people. I think theay need to go home and stay until theay learn how to give respect to the citizens which are paying them some of them. Look like theay just came off the farm. Theay recist and everything that go with it. I don't know who hire them but I know where I grew up can do better. If you have a brake in and call them theay get on the scene. Theay don't try to get no finger prints or nothing. I know one victim that told them he walked in his house, seen the man, ran out of the back door told them who he was and theay still did not pick him up. If theay had been working for the City when I was growing up. Theay would have been fired on the spot.

I don't know how many policemen you suppose to have for every thousand people but I am gong to found out. Ashburn do not have enough black police officers. What is wrong? I think why were can't get no job because of high taxes. I was told I don't know but most of you farmer's say blacks want work. They would rather have Mexican work because theay work 7 days a week from light to dark. Black's are not going to do that because most blacks go to church on Sundays.

The Mexican have got smart. Those over here legal will not work cheap. So theay will try and work the illegal but most of them are being deported. So its just a matter of time the more money the farmer's make the more theay want. But people are not going to work when I was a teenager we work cheap. We pick beans for 2 cents a pound. We pick cotton $2.50 to $3.00 per hundred. But that was in the 60's things were cheaper. Grocery as cheap but every year brought on a change. In the 80's things were better but the 90's were even better.

But look like things began to drag by the end of the 90's. Things was ok. I was working for Wal-Mart. I was making $8.00 per hour then 2000 came and 2004 look like the people got stuck with minimum wage $6.25 to $7.25 and Look like theay are married to $7.25 hour minimum wage.

But guess what $7.25 is not going to help the economy. If people don't have money to spend the economy is not going anywhere. What can you buy out of $7.25 after taxes, do the math. The president wants to raise the minimum wage but the R congress don't want to do that. So it is not the president it is congress.

So what are we going to do someone has to meet someone half way if not you ain't seen nothing yet. The congress don't want to raise the minimum wage but theay want to give them only a raise. I got married to a lovely young lady she was the love of my life. We had a good marriage for 29 years. She work at M & W Sportsware for a number of years. She loved me and I loved her. We had wonderful life. We did not fuss or fight. She was a sweet thing. My mother and father loved her like she was thair daughter.

Boy my mother would give me hell about her. Hold on. I had better tell you her sweet name Mrs. Alma L. Brown. I will never forget her. She was the lady of my dreams. I dated more girls but I did not marry any of them. I married the best lady I think. I lived in North Georgia for a while where a lot of pretty girls were. But I did not marry any of them. I came back when I grew up and married my wife.

We were married for 16 years and had not had any children's. But we were trying. And then my wife had a miscarriage and two years later guess what she got pregnant and on February 4, 1986, we had a baby girl. And guess what her name is Amery Renise Brown. Boy the family went wild. Theay said it took you all long enough. Boy she was my dad's everything. He would take her everywhere with him. Theay spoiled her rotten. Theay would go to the store. He would buy her ice cream and cookies and everything a granddad would buy for a little grandchild. Every Christmas theay would buy toys and dolls. Santa Claus would come to thaire house like he would to our house. I bet she had more toy's than any kid in the neighborhood.

We would go to church on Sunday and my wife would dress her just like her because she was a usher at our church and theay dressed in white. My mother would say look at my little grand girl. She is so pretty with her little white dress on. But about 3 years later, my dad became sick. I took him to the doctor and he got ok. So everyone was happy he began to play with is little pride and joy granddaughter. Amery and boy did he had his hands full. Boy she would get into trouble with me and her mother and run up to granddad because she knew if she made it to granddad, he would not let us spank her. My wife told your dad has that little girl spoil her. My wife told your dad has that little girl spoiled. He said this is my granddaughter and nobody touches her.

I told my dad you has spoiled her if I be the longest liver I will catch hell with her. This was in 1993 I did not know my dad was that sick. So when I taken him back to the doctor, that is when he called and said he wanted to talk with me. So we walked down the hall. He said your dad has about three months to live. I did not know what to say. So I said you are telling me my dad has three months? He said yes I said Dr. Anderson what he said. When Dr. Chang did surgery on him, he did not get all the cancer.

I said oh my God I ask the doctor could I get a second opinion? He said yes. So I taken him to Dr. Chang in Valdosta. I told him he did not get all the cancer and could he help my dad? But the pills was gong to cost him $300.00 apiece. I told Dr. Chang we could not afford them. So said he think. He knew when he could get them for free. And he did so dad began to take those pills and began to get better. This was in October. When I took him to the doctor in '93, those pill's was doing him good.

So by the last of November, dad began to moving slow I would say dad are you ok and he said yes why? I said nothing I just ask you know it's almost Christmas, it won't be long before Santa. He smile and said I am Santa. I say you better not tell your granddaughter that. He said boy you must think I crazy. I'm not going to tell her and nobody else. Better tell her. So I came in from work one evening and call him around 9:00 tonight at his home. So I began to think what is wrong know.

So when 9:00 p.m. came I called Dr. Chang and he asked had we discussed about getting a home care nurse to come around and see about my dad. I said no why? He said I thought I could help your dad, but the cancer has spread too far. He said you need to see those people because you all are going to need some help. After Christmas dad got bad off sick. He got so weak he could not walk unless you lifted him up on each side. I will never forget the look in his eyes that Sunday evening he reached his hand up just like he was trying to catch hold of someone's hand. And started calling his mother. He said mama. He was lying on his back in bed.

My dad passed away that Monday, January 27, 1994, so now I have to wake my mother up and tell her that dad had passed away. It broke my heart to wake my mother and wife and tell them dad had passed away. That was one of the hardest things I ever had to do. Also I had to wake my wife too. My daughter Ambery was only 7 years old when her grandad passed away but she loved him very much. My dad was like a friend and buddy I could talk to him about anything he would always tell me remember always try to do the right thing. Don't never try to take anything from anyone and don't let anyone take from you.

My dad is gone now and has been for a long time. I still miss him a lot. I also miss him from giving me hell when I would do wrong. He was a man among mens. He would give you the shirt off his back but if you rub him the wrong way, you was in trouble. Everybody in Ashburn and Turner County knew Jetty Brown. He was a hardworking man and he raised me up working just like he did. So I know about working because my dad had a pulpwood business for years. I ran the business. He also had a medical transport business. So when our driver need to be off, I drove the van I also ran a chain saw in the woods. I was the boss over the woods. But I worked like everyone else so I know what work is. Dad would always tell me don't ever borrow money from people you work for. Don't ever live in thaire house either. We all miss him because he would sit down and tell me a lot about Ashburn.

I don't know. I remember him telling me I wonder why Sylvester has the engine on the train and, mother, and we have the tail. He said that make Ashburn the ass. he is gone now I won't hear no more of his jokes so life must go on. I know he would want us to let go of him and love our lives. So after burying dad, mother, my wife and I was talking so mother said Jetty is gone.

I don't want to live in Ashburn anymore. I said mother all our people live in Ashburn. She said all I had is gone and she began to cry. My wife put her arm around her and said Cleve and Ambery are here. We finley got her calm down so she wanted to move. So I put in looking for a house over in Augusta, Georgia. I have a friend has been living over thaire for a long time. So I got with him and we started looking at houses and I found one not far from him so we decided we would take that one.

But we had to sell the two houses here. At that time, we had enough money to move. My wife had been going to the doctors at the medical college of Georgia Hospital for about ten years. So I knew a lot of people that work in security. I was already working security at Tifton Hospital. So one day my wife and I was talking about Augusta, but then my wife said you know I been thinking about our little girl. We haven't asked her how she would like moving over thaire.

So we ask Ambery and oh boy it was on. She start crying I don't want to move and leave all my friends. She said daddy please let's not move and leave granddaddy over here. By his self. So those few word's change everything. My mother said I had not thought about that. We will be leaving Jetty over here by his self. So when mother said that, I know we were not going to move.

My wife Alma said the crime rate is higher than it is in Atlanta. Alma said I would not want to raise my daughter up in the big city no way. So all our plans changed. About three years later my wife, Alma became ill. She had been going to the doctor's at M-C-G for treaments. So it went on for a while. She would be doing good for long time then she would be in so much pain. Cancer will tear a family apart. I don't wish that on nobody we were almost to get over my dad and then Alma became. But we knew one day it would catch up with her so it did.

Cancer cost me a lot first of all it cost me my wife and my home a lot of sleepless nights all the money we had saved caused my daughter to be raised from 11 years old by her father Cleveland without a mother. That is why I give to any kind of cancer drive because I had the chance to know what it do to a family so when you see them having anything for the cancer society give freely. It is for a good cause.

When you are a working father trying to raise an 11 year old girl without a mother, it is hard and she is in school. I did not know anything about doing little girl's hair.

My wife passed away November 22, 1997. My mother would help me all she could but she was in her 80's. But she almost needed someone to help her. Little did I know three years later I would be putting my mother in a nursing home. But before I put her thaire, I met this lady and we started dating. She had two girls theay was a little older than my daughter and before I knew what was going on, she had moved her and her kid's in without asking me anything so I got angry and I told my daughter theay got to go because I had never lived with a woman in my life. I was raised better than that.

She said daddy, let them stay so she looked she was happy and I sure cold use a lady's help with her and myself by now. So everything was on time this was around 1999 I had dated more ladies but theay were from out of town. Theay just wanted to have some fun. Not help me raise my daughter. But this lady Mrs. D., she knew me my family , me and her dad was good friend's also her mother too. So when she moved in with us, she did me a big favor.

Because she hope me raise my daughter up to where she could do for herself. Even though we not togeather anymore, I will help her anyway I can. I meet up with her in the store. We are still friends, but sometimes you know the best of friends have to part. But we are not mad with each other. So that's the good part she told me she had married the guy was living with. I told her I wish them well.

But I can't help but to think about some of the things my dad did. I rember when I use to drank he was getting at me about dranking. I made this mistake and ball my fist up at him. Boy, he knock me out cold. Guess what, I never did it again.

My friend Diane and her girls I will never forget them. Her girl's Nickie and Magain took Ambery as thaire little sister. My mother was crazy about Diane and her girls because Diane hope me so much with Ambery because mother was old she did the best she could. But it took a younger woman because she had to do Ambery's hair every morning and get her ready to catch the bus for school. And that is why Diane and her girls are in this book because theay earn the right to be in here. By helping me and Ambery and my mother.

I can't remember the date in the year 2005 I admitted my mother to Ashburn Health Care. So theay took us around to look at everything and I ask how did she like it. She said fine. At this point I did not dream of my mother staying out thaire 11 years. But when she first got thaire for a long time she was doing good. I visit out thaire every day some time at night to see how everything was working out. She was doing well walking around.

So I was okay with that because the reason I put her out thaire was because her mine was bad. She would forget and would get up 3 o'clock in the morning and come down to my house. So I had to get somebody to stay with her in the daytime because I had to work and Ambery had to go to school and the girls. Diane was working. She was a home care nurse. So everybody was away in the day time. So I had to get someone to stay with her in the day time.

So I got Betty Shine. She would come down every morning or I would go pick her up before I go to work. So Finally she got so bad that I calling all her brother in Ohio and her sister in Miami and told them what was going on. So theay told me to do what was best for me and my mother. Theay said she is only our sister. She is your mother and you have the last say so over her. So I begin to check on places to put her and decided to put her here in Ashburn where it would be easy on the family to go and visit her.

For the first five years she was doing fine. Everybody worked out thaire knew her. So as time went by she was doing fine. I went to see her every day. I felt good about what I had done. I did not have to worry about her leaving home at night or running away in the daytime. As the years went by, things began to change, but I should have been looking for that because when I put mother out thaire she was 80 years old. This was in 2000. She got where she could not walk. I told them about giving her medicine and theay said she don't want to take it. She has rights just like you and she don't want to take it.

When a person's mind has gone bad, she can't make no decisions for herself. I begin to have some doubts and I would had listen to my daughter and moved her from out thaire she might be alive today. But that was all in God's plan. So all the people I trusted out thaire let me down. I would go out thaire every day and feed her before she got bad sick. Me and my daughter would go to meetings out thaire at Christmas time. We would go shopping Mother's Day, Valentine all those kind of card's. Amery got where she would say daddy I hate to see grandmother like that. I love her so much and she would start to cry. And I would say hay you are a grown young lady you are not supposed to cry. But I know it hurt her because it hurt me too.

I had a sweet mother because if I needed something I could go to mother and get it. I could go to dad but he want to ask a whole lot of questions like for what. When you going to pay me back and all that stuff. But he would let me have it. But mother, it was okay, all right. My mother was a member at Mt. Olive Baptist Church for years. One lady from church to my knowing came out a few times to visit my mother was Mrs. Rose Mary Hall. If it was anymore I don't know the pastor's. Theay had while my mother was in the nurse home not a one went to visit her. My dad was a member. My wife was an usher thaire. Her health fail and she could not attend. Me and my daughter moved our membership.

I can remember on my birthday mother would ask me what you want for your birthday. I would say a cake and she would say yes a jelly cake. Then she would tell my dad Jetty take me up town where I can get the stuff to make Cleveland my baby a birthday cake. My dad would say Arlean that old grey man ain't no baby no more my mother would say I don't care if he is still my baby. And she would bake me a cake.

Those are the kind of things you miss but all the years she was in the nursing home I only missed about 5 times from going to visit her. She got where she could not talk. She would just look at you and smile. My daughter would ask her grandma do you know who I am? She would just look at her and smile. My mother was a good mother. I know the doctor say she had a lot of mini stroke's that is what caused her to lose her speech. She got like that about the 5th or 6th year she was out thaire. She begin to go down.

She would do good and then she would stop eating then theay would call me. I would go out thaire. I found out people of all age is not going to eat as fast as 50 and 60 year old people's. People 80 years old and above are like them. You got some people working at nursing homes just to say theay have a job. But if you don't care about older people you are in the wrong place and the time my mother spent at Ashburn Health Care, I found out some of the certified assistants and nurses did not care about the patients.

I would be out thaire to visit my mother, the phone would ring, theay would just sit thaire and look at it. I would say hay you not going to pick it up. The nurse would say theay don't want nothing. I told her now I see what happen when I call out here and no one pick's up the phone.

During 2010 I did not say anything to Ambery but I could see mother was failing I could look at her skin color but I just went on and did not want to except the fact that my mother whom I love very much who nurse me from a baby who took care of me all my life when I was sick was slowly slipping away from us. Mother made it through 2010 by the grace of God. I just said on new years thank you Lord for letting my mother stay with us a little longer. Little did I know that Jesus had plans for mother on the other side. But I just want to think the Lord for letting her stay with us 96 years. She lived a long life and a good life.

My late dad Mr. Jetty Brown and mother had been married almost 60 years when my dad past away. In 1994 he was 79 years old. He was a hard working man he also grew up in Ashburn. The good Lord was so good to my mother that he called her home on April 23, 2o11 to be with him. So me and Ambery have had a rough time trying to at least to being without her the Lord is able. We get stronger every day. Mother had four sister's and three brothers all gone before her. She has one sibling left. Her baby brother who is James C. Mathis. He is on the picture with me and Sam we three grew up together in Ashburn and we was bad to the bone.

Thaire is nobody left but me and my two daughters, Ambery and Merchelle but life must go on. But I miss them all very much. Ambery finish High School. Now she is in college. Mother has been gone over 2 years now. So I guess she is with my wife and father and her sister and brothers and I know theay are all happy. We are doing okay out of all we have been through the Lord is able.

So I don't have many kinfolk on my mother's and father's side. Where I grew up in Ashburn. So I guess I ride it out. My roots are here and some friends are here. But if I was about 25 years younger, I might would pull up and leave. I want my daughter to leave because Ashburn does not have anything to offer young black people.

It is not like when I was growing up. The town is gone down. No stores to buy anything except Dollar General and Fred's and that is it. So if you have to buy shoes or dress shirts, anything look worth anything, you have to go to Tifton or Cordele and most of the people live here in Ashburn work in Tifton. But Ashburn I don't believe will ever come back and stores open up because you got people with money holding up progress. Theay say theay want this and theay want that but you are not doing anything to bring Ashburn back to life.

Ashburn will never be like it once was. We don't have no jobs. People are hurting now worse than theay were in 1952. We just had a doctor's clinic to close because theay was not getting enough business. And could not get any doctor's here to work thaire. But we have one clinic left. If you looking for a place to come to after you retire, and live and not have to pay all your money on clothes and rent, Ashburn is ok to live in. But don't look for no fancy night club or big shopping malls or big Wal-Mart, but you can go 20 miles South or 20 miles north and find either one.

You know long time ago Ashburn where I grew up had just about everything to offer and that haven't been no 50 years ago, but we had a lot of people leave. Some moved to Tifton and Cordele. Most of them what still work. Theay work in those town so theay say it would be better for them to move thaire. I guess theay are right because we have the highest gas prices in the state of Georgia so theay are right it is better for them to move. And some moved to Florida but me I guess I will live the rest of my life out here. Mother and dad and wife and a lot of kinfolk are bury here.

It is August 27, 2013 as I write this book about me growing up in Ashburn and Turner County. I raise my baby girl Amery here right now. We have I would say about 4,000 or 5,000 people in the city. But in all city and county, we have about 9,000 or 10,000 people. Don't hold me to that but I think I'm right but we can't get any jobs to come here. I don't know what the young people are going to do. We have interstate 75 coming right by our back door and still we are not doing any better.

Ashburn once have had 12,000 people here in the early days. But like myself and a white friend of mine, Wayne Blue, we both or about the same age. I think we know more about the history about Ashburn than anybody so far. We can help one another because he know things I don't know and I know thing he don't know. I just wanted to put that in this book.

My cousin Sam Hampton who has pass away and my Uncle James C. Mathis who live in Miami, Florida, all three of us grew up in Ashburn together. Sam lived here until he passed away in 2010. So I have a lot of time invested in Ashburn but I don't know weather in Ashburn growing up was a whole lot better back then because you had jobs you could find work.

You could walk home at night from the movie and not be stopped by the police. You could walk to the store and not be stopped and ask where are you going. But know everything has change so I guess I grew up in the best time. The kids of today theay get more than I got when I was a teenager some of them have a car at 16. I could not get a car until I was grown. But no mom and dad buy them a car, put the gas in the car, make the car payments and pay the insurance. And theay go to school but when theay get out of school and mom and dad tell them about tell the about getting a job.

So now I am going back to when I was growing up you know when you are an only child you get most anything you want. My dad bought me a guitar from the Western Auto. It was run by Mr. Al Butler on College Street. I played with that thing and could never learn how to play it. My dad had a friend he could play a guitar so he was going to teach me how to play. Man I never learn how to play it so I let Sonny kept it and he tore it up. But he told me he would pay me for it. Forgot about it.

Fifteen years later he came to Albany to visit his sister and drove over to Ashburn to see my dad. I was grown man by then. He paid me twice as much as the thing cost. I didn't know what to say. He said you thought I had forgot didn't you? I said yes sir. He said I had to leave in a hurry when I left Albany and I thanked him and I never seen him anymore. I think he died up thaire but at least he paid me for the guitar.

You know it is 2013 and Ashburn has nothing to offer the young people. No jobs, no recreation, not even a swimming pool. So when you got so much leisure time, nothing to do, theay are going to get into something. So we can't fault the kids. Fault the so called leaders for not have in job training programs to train these young people for these jobs.

When we elect people in office for a reason not for you to just sit up thaire and say I am a elected official. And get a check every month. You are up thaire to make a change. We have three black city council and theay can't show me one thing theay have done since theay been up thaire. Not one that is bad when Ashburn the City is 60% black. I just don't understand why things are like theay are. We going backwards. This late in time I thought things is supposed to be getting better but I don't know.

Thing was not this bad in the 50's and 60's. I don't know if something don't change 20 years from now Ashburn where I grew up won't be nothing but sidewalks and parks. I think Ashburn need more than we need grocery stores.

I know one thing we don't need is all these murders we have had in Ashburn and Turner County. We have had countless murders in the last ten years. The late one was on September 7, 2013. If something isn't done it will be dangerous to walk the street where I grew up. Our young black male's don't have jobs and job's want come here for reasons we don't have a hospital is one reason and a lot more.

I think the reason we are having so much black on black violence because we don't have enough black's in the police department or Sheriff department. We have one or two in the police department and one in the Sheriff Department. We need more African American in both departments. Black officer can do more with African American than white officer. I know because I have seen it happen if thaire is a fight. And the police is call to the scene and when theay get thaire the first thing theay do is cursing and calling names such as the N word and if you got a large gathering of black people the N word special if some has been drinking.

That is just like pouring gas on a fire.

If you have enough black officer when something like that happen, you can dispatch a black and white officer because the black officer is not afraid. Because when he drive up and get out theay will began to tell him what happen. He already know if he get out cussing he is not going to get any help from the people. He know this. Why because he is one of us. That is why he can arrest blacks.

Without any trouble he don't get out of the car cussing and that is difference between the white officer and the black officer. Cussing is not going to make blacks afraid of you. Because it don't make me afraid. We just want help you.

I don't know why we don't have any black police officer here. Only two, one part time and one female in the office. I don't know why when theay come here theay stay a while and leave. I don't know whether it is the pay or what. Or whether it's the good old boy system. But whatever it is theay want stay long. Same with the Sheriff department, both department might need to be looked into. I t's a lot of stuff go on in both department. I may be wrong but I think both departments hire just enough black's to not get caught for discrimination. I might be wrong but that is what I think what theay are doing.

If theay solve this murder what was done on September 7, 2013, it will be the first one that I know of since I been grown. We have murders when I was growing up here but the law would catch who did it and theay would go to prison for a long time. And another thing, back thein when theay put you in jail, nobody would come up thaire the next day trying to get you out. If it was murder, the law would not even talk to you about it until later.

You don't have good law officers anymore. The only thing ride around go the café sit around drink coffee back up under a shade tree in the summer time in two cars and talk to one another. I seen it a lot of times when I worked for the city those five and ½ years.

Now a lot of people back when I was growing up here in Ashburn we had a lot of respect for our older people. Today our young people has none. When I was growing up you did not hear young people using curse words. If a young kid used a bad word and the neighbor heard you and told your mother, boy it was on. And please don't tell dad boy you got a shinning and I bet you did not say it anymore.

I can remember when we were on the farm in Sibley, my job was when I get home from school. First pull off your school clothes, get something to eat, you seek back then we had wood stoves. So I had to take the stove wood in the house in the kitchen. You see we had in our kitchen two wood boxes we put the stove wood in. So I knew that was my job after school before I got to play.

But even back then kids would sometime forget to do what theay are suppose to do. You know what I forgot, but guess what? When dad got through with me, I did not forget anymore. I remember another time I was suppose to water the hogs, I forgot. But did not forget to put his belt on my back in! But I thank them for every whipping theay gave me it made me a better man.

You know Ashburn has a lot of black history here. But now to get it I don't know because most of all the older black's has passed on. I can rember growing up in Ashburn, it was a lot of working going on in Ashburn and Turner County you had Mr. Harry Bell's packing shed on East Washington about where Kett is. You could get a job thaire packing tomato plants. Also Reinhard'ts farms cabbage plants and onion plants. Ashburn had it going on back then. I did a little research and found out that the housing project on Stevens Street is named after a black highly respected man. Manson Payne as well as one of the pioneer citizens of Ashburn.

When I lived in North Georgia, I work for Southeastern Construction Company out of Snellville, Georgia. The owner of the company was E.R. Snell. The town was named after him. That's where I work. When I first went to North Georgia, I did a lot of work on I-20 from Atlanta to Augusta when 20 get almost to Augusta it turns into the Bobby Jones Expressway I don't know how far the express way go beyond Augusta that's as far as I been on it. That was in 1961 I think when I work on that road.

I lived in Austell, Georgia before I went to Calhoun, Georgia that's where I lived until I came back to this town where I grew up. That was a bad mistake I made. I got stuck here and married my wife of 29 years until she passed away in 1997. So my mistake turn into a beautiful wife and a pretty daughter. This is 2013 and she is 27 years old. And daddy would not take anything for her. I have another daughter by a lady I was courting before I married my wife. I think she is 43 so you see God has a way of making something you think is bad turn into something good.

Here I am writing this book. I am 75 years old. I never thought when I was young I would live to get this old. But when you young, you don't think much about anything but girls having a good time. You don't think about life dying or none of those things. But as you get older, you wonder where did the time go. Then you start thinking oh man, its getting late in my life. I need to do something. Your hair start turning gray, your think how good God has been to you down through the years. He could have taken me anytime he wanted to and he still can now. But I think him for letting me live a little longer. God is a good God.

And I think him every day. But where I grew up in Ashburn, if the people don't change one of these days, God is going to send something through here. Thaire is too much hate in Ashburn, Georgia, people can see it and so can I. It is so stupid to let skin color cause you to go to hell. Tell me what color are the people in the Bible. I know you have one with the pictures in it. Things are much difference now you can walk at night unless you are stop by the law.

People have got so lazy theay don't want to walk anywhere I guess that is why we have so many fat people. I don't believe we had them many fat and that is bad for your health. It is mostly the young people. Theay don't care what theay eat. That is not good. Theay will have health problems. But I can't say much about eating because I love to eat but I don't get fat. I have not got fat in all these years. It is no fatness standard weight so I don't worry about finding clothes to fit me or shoes.

Growing up I never through Ashburn would go down with more people and jobs. I never dream Ashburn would be in the shape it is in. What happen?

Ashburn is nothing I had visioned it would be when I grew up to be a man. I had told some of the kids when we get to be men Ashburn will be a large place and we will have a lot of job's. And a lot of people will be here theay were here for a while but where did theay go. And why Ashburn was not suppose to be like this. We don't have anything here why we need all these parks?

We need some one in leadership who can revive Ashburn but who will it be? Some people don't like the way Ashburn is and some don't care. Because theay got rich when Ashburn was up and running working people for nothing and still is. Some people say nothing is coming here. We had a cotton gin in town we had a tomato plant shed. Where theay pack tomato plants we had a couple of sawmills. We had a greyhound bus station we had a black pool hall and Barber shop down town. You had more people here than we do now and had more job's then than we do now and had more job's then than we do now. We had a freezer locker down 41 South where we could buy fresh meat and everything you could buy fresh beef and pork. We also had two hardware stores. We also had two farm tractor dealerships in Ashburn. We had three jewelry stores.

We also had a hot dog stand. We also had two or three TV repair shops. I told you earlier in the book the movie place burned down. Where I grew up we also had a Coca Cola bottle in Ashburn.

I am not saying this because I used to work for him but Lamar Whiddon was the best sheriff Turner County ever had he elected to five terms and served nearly seventeen years until his death in 1993. Thaire will never be another not in this lifetime. Ashburn had a lot of good people. So I guess that is what kept where I grew up alive. But I guess those good people died out Ashburn died with them. We also had a train depot built in the 1930's.

The young people of today theay eat chicken but I bet that theay have never been to where theay raise the chicken theay need to go to those chicken houses and see all those chickens in them. And then theay will know how theay are raised. Everybody is talking about Obama Care will cost but nobody has showed me how much it would cost. And the difference between the insurance theay have now and Obama Care. I think if insurance is going to be cheap enough for poor people to buy it I don't think it is going to be high.

I think I am going to tell you all about October 31, me and my grandad Will Brown's shotgun. I had seen the gun sitting at the head of dad's gun rack, and he said don't mess with that gun. I said ok, and that was it. But one day I was in the house by myself and pick it up. Luckily it was not loaded because I pull the trigger and snap. And I keep doing it because I loved to hear it snap so I put it down before mom and dad came in the house. And ran and got on my bike and started riding.

If we were living on the farm at Sibley, Georgia about 8 miles north of Ashburn. On the William's Farm. I ask my dad why someone cut the barrel off. He said a dirt dobber made a nest in the barrel and when grandad shot it , it split the barrel and he had to cut if off. One Sunday morning mother was outside taken in clothes off the clothes line what she had washed. And dad was out to the barn feeding the mules. I was supposed to be in bed but I had got up and was playing with the shotgun, but I did not know the gun was loaded. I pick it up pointed it at the ceiling and pull the trigger and boom and it kicked and knocked me down. Dad and mom came running in the house. It was full of smoke. Dad said boy I told you not to mess with that gun. I said a fly lite on me and flew to the ceiling and I was trying to kill it. Dad said that's ok. Pull that little shirt off.

I remember when we lived on the farm in the early 50's we had a store across the creek where we lived. So my mother sent me to the store to get some sugar and rice. Down at the creek was a foot log you had to walk across the water. Now some of you young people don't know what a foot log is. It's a round piece of trunk of a tree is called a log. You lay it across a stream of water. That is called a foot log. I walk that log a many of days going to school and to the store.

I did not even have a bicycle because we were too poor. You know people did not know what food stamps was. It wasn't any in those days. People died because theay could not afford insurance. Back then it was no such thing like Medicare, Medicaid. If it had been a lot of poor people would have lived.

I see the young people of today in 2014. Theay just don't know how much theay are blessed. The way theay are today could not have made it because when our parent told us something to do, we did it with no back talk but now in these times look like children are telling the parent what to do. But you know people change. But when I was coming up nothing changed. The parent meant what theay said last week and the same the next week. Theay did not change. You might would have to change clothes when theay got through with you. You can tell all of us that was raised back I the early 50's. Because our parent raised us we did not raise our parent ok. I am so glad my parents raised me. I thank them today. Theay both are gone now, but I love them both. But God loved them the most and he carried them back home with him.

I will never forget the man that first learned me how to drive. His name was Everett Willliams. My dad called him Shag. He lived on the Williams Farm at Sibley, Georgia too. Mr. Shay drove tractor on the farm so one day he was passing our house. I went out in the yard and stop him and ask him would he learn me how to drive and he said yes. But you have to ask your dad if he don't mind. I will learn you how to drive. My dad told him he did not care. So the learner process begin.

The tractor he drove was a Farmall tractor. I would be waiting for him every evening to come by the house. He would hold me in his lap and let me drive down to the gate. So when he through I was ready to handle it by myself he would show me how to put it in a slow gear and I would drive it to the gate. I keep on until I told him to put it in a faster gear.

Then I was ready to try my dad's old car. I will never forget dad had a 1940 Chevrolet, he would let me drive down to the mailbox. I was on the main big road when we would come from Ashburn. He would let me

Moonshine and Living in the Deep South

drive from the mailbox to the house. From then on I as on my way to driving a car. You know the children's of today would not made it back then. No I'll take that back theay would have made it because it was such thing as child abuse. If it had been our parents as strong theay would have protested it. But you know at this time in age this is 2014. We passed the 50's and 60's but the new laws this country have now theay have it where the parent can't make them mine. You know a parent is not going to hurt thaire children the law don't want the parent to make them mine. Theay want to send them to prison.

I can remember my ad sent me down in the woods to the whiskey still to et a flash light he had left thaire the night before. I should had gone and got the light and come on back but instead I was down thaire playing around and broke 3 -5 gallon jug's wasted about 50 pounds of sugar. And the bad part about the whole thing I did not tell my dad. He went down thaire to check the other stuff to see how near it was or was it ready.

That's when he found out what I had done. I tried to lie out of it. He said no. Because it's only four people know where this still is you myself Smith and Ralph. Not even the man who owned the place. He say you might as well tell the truth. If you don't, I am going to beat the hell out of you. Then I thought I better tell the truth because this big black man is mad. I better tell him and sure enough he almost beat hell out of me. But after that he told me he did not beat me for braking the jugs or the sugar he said I whop your ass because you tried to lie to me about it. When I knew only four people's knew where it was. He would tell me always tell the truth.

I have learned it is easy to tell the truth because you don't have to tell it but one time my dad told a liar is dangerous. He said if you don't never tell the first lie you are all right. But where you get in trouble when you tell the first one you have to lie to cover everyone you tell. So after a while no be leaves you. So I found out if you don't tell the first one you are in good shape. So I often think about the things my dad taught me about lies. And stay in shape where you can be your own man. Don't do anything where another man can hold it against you. Stand tall and furm in what you beleave in.

Growing up I Ashburn and Turner county going to Eureka High School, I had teacher's like Mr. Dye. Mrs. King, Mrs. Hayse. Mr. Andrews, Mr. Burke, Mr. Blastingale, Mrs. Rose Jackson, Mrs. Jones and Mr. Jackson and of course the King.

Mr. Hodge King who we all loved so much. He was all our king and daddy. Turner County will never have another King like Hodge. All of us old students still have a lot of respect for all of our teachers that taught at Eureka. We will never forget the good old days at Eureka. Eureka and its teacher took young men and women and made grown men and women out of them. Today I am in my 70's and I have just as much respect today as I did when I was in school. I look at them today as I did when I was in school. I look at them today and think them for what theay done for me.

You know back then we did not have nothing. We played basketball on a clay court. We had used and torn school book's some had been mark all in. But Mr. King would go to then the all-white school and beg some time. Theay would give him what he wanted and sometime theay would not. But he did not give up. Theay would do him just like congress are doing the President. Ad this is 2013 so you see nothing has changed. That was back in the Jim Crow days. Theay called it back thein. Today theay call it racism. It's the same thing. The word's difference but it mean the same. So you see over 50 years and more we as black people are still catching hell. We had republican back thean and we have them now nothing change.

This is why our President is catching hell in the white house now. You have some of those racist congressmen in Washington. Don't want a black man to tell them what to do. Not even the President of the U.S.A.... How do that make our country look to other countries? I am not and I have never seen a president treated like this one. What is it?

He has been cussed at, call names, talked about. We have had presidents that has done worse thean this president. Theay was not treated like this President. I don't care what nobody say, I am a black man. I know what the problem is. Obama is black and in congress you have congressmen from the South. The son's of Jim Crow racist Klan don't like black people.

And no one wanted to fight just have fun now. I will tell you more about dad and Smith's liquor later on. It is 2013 and the government has shut down. It shut down October 4, 2013. You know our country should be glad to have a black president. But the people some of them are not. Most of the whites are not. But we the blacks are very happy to have one of our own in the white house. But from day one the republication said theay would not help him do anything and theay did just that.

Out of all you have done to us in Ashburn and everywhere else you don't want a black man to tell you what to do but look my white brother get over it is going to happen. So if you don't like it leave the country. It is payback time. You are going to see a lot of Obama's. Theay are growing up every day.

The white man why are you so mad with the black man. Right here where I grew up, blacks have been killed by whites and to this nothing has been done. I know when we lived in the housing project a black girl was raped by a white boy. Guess what? Nothing was done. But this same boy went out in the country and raped a white house wife. Guess what he went to prison for a very long time. So, you guys should not be mad with the black man. But out of all you guys have done to us, we have had our woman's killed and our brother's, father's, and grandfather's lynched right here in the south Georgia.

Oh yes we can. Things are changer. I might not live to see it. But right here in Ashburn. What is of Ashburn Black's will be running it. But you probably will be gone like myself. But your kids and grandkids will be working for some blacks and want think anything about it. Money is the same color. So we parents what are living now in 2013 need to be teaching our children how to get along with the other race of people. Not hate I got up town and I look at some of the white men have hate written all over thair face. Theay some of them hate to see a black man talking with a black man. You know what theay them nigger lovers I have heard that statement made in stores.

And one more thing I cannot understand why is gas so high in Ashburn. In Ashburn thain Tifton. We don't have any one here to check that out. I guess theay don't care. But long time ago the people back then would have check it out.

The problem is Ashburn today your so called leaders don't lead any more theay follow. But I can tell you now if you are black and try to get a job in Ashburn you are out of luck. I have heard this more times than a little. The young people want work the reason theay want work is because you want hire them. No wonder no jobs will come here the have heard how the race relation is and theay are not going to come to place like that.

No one is going to come here. You can build parks form here to Atlanta. That's not going to do Ashburn any good. I hate to say this about where I grew up. I think it is beyond help. You know Ashburn was once a nice place to live. You could find a job anywhere. People was people back thain. Not a wolf in sheep clothes. But people don't care anymore.

I thought the people in this country would be glad of our president but I was wrong. I think some of the people up north and all of the white people in the south see anybody be president than to see someone black. What a shame. I wonder what you all's forefather would say about its children today. We as black people have never been respected as people or citizens of the U.S.A. We had everything that our Anstister's owned took and stolen from us by the white man. Just like the Indians.

And now you would not believe what I'm about to tell you our fore the Mexican are being treated better than we black's are being treated. Our ansisters hope build this country with sweat and blood. Some of us was in slave and work like mules. Some was beaten some was lynched but we are still denied the respect that we deserve. Our foreparents land was taken just like the Indian by the white man.

It makes me mad when I hear a white man say he work hard for what he's got. That is the biggest lie his parent took it from some poor black family. So what goes up, comes down. Rember what goes around comes around. We as black American has never been treated right. We have been put in jail for no reasons. We have been put in prison behind lies. But do you think we should love someone who has caused us so much pain?

God say we are to love everybody. He said you are to love your enemy as well as your friend. But your friend would not put us through all this. We have been put through by our white brothers. Look what happen in Florida in 1923. A white women's lie caused a lot of black men to be lynched. By saying she had been beat up and possible rape. The white men went wild. Theay found a black man and lynched him that was not enough. Theay set him on fire and burn him to stake. Theay did not try to found out anything from the woman theay went all over that little town killing black's.

I did not read anywhere. The police or N law in that county tried to do anything about it. So that make me think that they was a part of it. Ninety six years ago when I read part of the story I could not beleave that we live in a country would allow something like to happen even back in 1923 and no one was punished for the crime.

About 70 or 80 years later, the state of Florida compensated the families that were lynched so that let me know that the state of Florida knew what was going on and would not do anything about it. You cannot put a price on human life. White people think theay can buy anything with money that is what going to take them to hell. What happen in Florida 96 years ago was the worse thing I ever heard in my life.

I know bad things has been happen to us all over the U.S.A. I have been told a lot of stores about Ashburn by my great uncle when he was alive and I was growing up here. I rember the one he told me about ta a man call Mr. Nance who cut hair he had a shop in a place here in town what theay called Gabe Quarters. He was killed after he closed his shop on his way home. He was also robbed and stuffed in a sewage pipe. No one every found out who killed him. So you see Ashburn has a track record of black people being killed and nobody know who done it or nobody tries to found out.

We had a young man named Robert Martin who was killed out at the Old Eureka School off Hwy. 112 in West Ashburn. And nobody was ever charged for that murder. We have several murders in Ashburn and Turner county nobody has been with them. We have more young black men in prison in the State of Georgia I believe than any state in the Union, but one day about these murders in Ashburn and Turner County and somebody is going to pay for them you can sweep stuff under the rug for so long until you can't get any more up under it. And thean the truth will come out.

We have a man who came to Ashburn by the name of Jim Hedges and his wife Joan Hedges from Florida. And he became mayor of the city. He has served almost two turns as mayor and he has done a good job for the city as a whole. He has done an exlant job in West Ashburn. We have a new water tank, new fire station and a new EMS station. And we also has solar panels.

You know sometime the Lord has to take stumble blocks out of the way before a town can get what it needs. The West side of the city has never been treated fair like the up keep of the roads and streets. Hay don't take my word for it, get in your car and ride over thair and you will see. And then ride on the East side look at the ditches on the East side and look at the ones on the West Side. I can't understand, the people pay tax on the West side of Ashburn. Just like the people on the East side. The money is the same color. But at the end of the day, it goes back to city hall.

And the city council to let this kind of stuff go on the supervisor of the street department should be held accountable for it but nobody say anything. So it is 2013 and racism still live in this little town where I grew up, but all white people are not like that because I don't believe my friend Ben Baker and his staff at the Wiregrass are like that. No more and his staff at the wiregrass are like that. No more people than it is in Ashburn, we should get along like brothers and sisters because we are. And ain't nothing we can do about it is thaire?

When we first moved up to Sibley on the William Farm, daddy not have a car so we would go over to his bro-law Charlie Fields and we would ride to Ashburn with him and Aunt Luey. If not that his other two bro-laws lived about one half mile down at Dakota. Where theay both worked on the Southern Railroad. Uncle C.D. had a car Uncle George did not.

Sometime we would go to Ashburn on the train because we could ride with Aunt Ozie and Uncle Georgie and it would not cost anything because we worked for the railroad and we could ride on his pass and I loved that. Some time I would go down to Aunt Ozie's on Friday, stay all night. Just to get a chance to ride the train to Ashburn that Saturday.

It was a lot of more kid's lived up thair on the farm where we lived wanted to ride the train like me but could not because theay did not have a uncle like I did working for the railroad. I would brag about it. Theay could have got thaire parent to ride them. I don't know why none of them would not catch the train with us. But you all know what. Thats been a long time ago. You know what I have not been on a train since right up 41 Highway at Dakota. Where we would catch it at. But all of my aunts and uncles, and my parents are gone. In just want to dedicate this book to all of them and all of the people mention in this book.

It's October 9, 2013 and we have two government fussing over tax money. The city and county. The Bible say it is not a sin to have money but to lust or love money. That is when you get in trouble so that whit I think happen to these two governments. Man this little town where I grew up has the whole State of Georgia looking at Ashburn and Turner county in Superior court. The County's specially hired attorney said the commission was willing to let the tax end. Well what is all the fuss is about. But Chairman McCard said the county dose not want the tax to end. Well what we have here. The attorney say one thing and the chairman say another so what is it county. You eather do or do not want the tax.

In other words', court can't decide how the sales tax is split up. It must be decided by the county commission and city council. Myself as a writer for the newspaper, I don't know where it go from here. I was talking with one city councilman and he told me if the tax ended the City would have to raise (x) amount of dollars. And theay would have to find a way theay would have to cut some programs. Or go up on taxes, or go up on utilities. And all of this is bad. We, the taxpayers, did not create this problem, and I don't think we should suffer because two governments could not sit down like mens and work this out. Now with the government shut down people are unemployed no jobs here and people cannot raise taxes or anything else because theay have not been too long ago theay raised utilities. I just don't see people paying money.

This should have never went to court. Now it has cost the county tax payers and city tax payers money because the city tax payers pay count tax to and now the city are saying theay may have to go up on things or raise taxes. I think you will see a lot of people moving out of Ashburn. Those who own homes here will be trying to sell them. And where I grew up, will be a ghost town. And I am sure I would move too because we are already paying more utilities than Tifton and where I live we have to pay all the utilities out here.

But in Tifton, some of thair apartments the company pays some of your utilities. But theay don't at Annadale Parks. But in this small town, the people with the money control the town. It is like that in all small towns in Southwest Georgia.

But guess what, the young people are not going to put up with it. Those that live here are leaving. I cannot blame them because thaire is no future for the young blacks. Because what few jobs here that pay anything the whites have them all the blacks can do is work at these fast food places and making $7.25 per hour and that want take care of a baby. You know I just sit and watch things and listen. You know my parent always told me to look and listen.

All my adult life, since I been grown I have seen the white man think he has all the brain and we don't have any. Look at the speaker of the House John Boehner supposed to have a lot of sense but he is letting these no good people from the southern tea party states telling him how to do his job. But guess what? Obama is not going to let Boehner or the Tea party to tell him how to run the White house. Because he know what he is doing. And if Boehner and Congress would do what theay were elected to do, we would not have this shut down.

But theay are trying to hurt the President but what theay fail to look at Obama was put thaire by God. And he is on a mission and it is not going anywhere until it is finished so all you white people say you love the Lord. But you hate the president. I heard of one big white church in Turner County on Sundays that is all theay pastor talk about the president. Don't he know God sees everything he do and here everything he say. Do he not know that? What kind of preacher is that? But he is going to give in account for his action.

You know I had a white friend here that ran a dry cleaner here but he has pass away. And he told me one day I went in to pick up a shirt from the cleaner. He said Cleve you black need to wake up every time you see these white people at the church theay are not having church. Theay are having a meeting about you all. He said I was born and raise here. Blacks have never been treated right and I don't care who know I told you. I told him that I knew that we was not treated right. If I didn't like I would not tell you this. You tell your daddy jetty what I told you.

So even back in the 60's and 70's, thaire was some good white people. But now you can't found many men in like Mr. D.P. You can found some that will smile in your face and put a knife in your back. I thought it would be better by now.

On this beautiful Sunday afternoon. It is 4:25 p.m. October 13, 2013. I was thinking back when I was growing up here all the stores we had. I rode down in Ashburn this morning not to town because everything is closed all the stores are falling in at the top but some of them the front look good. But drive through the alleys and you will see what I am talking about.

I live out East of town next to the Interstate. Where I live when I was growing up was nothing but woods and Interstate 75 Highway did not exist. Nothing existed but highway 112 and woods. But now when you get past where Shinglers mule barn was you have stores on both sides of the road but that is not Old Ashburn most of those stores are new businesses.

All the way to Interstate 75 Highway. On both sides of the state route 112 highway. Go all the way to Rebecca. Here in Ashburn people are still moving and we have the highest gas prices in the state and high taxes. For one thing in the few stores here the prices are two or three times too high so we drive 20 miles and still save money most of your stores here are owned by Indians. When I was growing up here I would have dreams Indians would own any stores in Ashburn. At first I could not beleave it what happen to all the white people what owned stores here. Where did theay go?

Did our government let them have the money to buy the stores? Yes, and if I went to the bank tomorrow, my credit would be good enough my credit might not be high enough when I was growing up here people did not know what credit scores was all you had to do was have good credit. I think this was some smart Republication idea to keep poor blacks from borrowing money from the banks. Because theay knew back thein theay was not paying them enough to live off let lone pay a bank note. So theay made it hand thean for us to get a loan and guess what theay are doing the same thing in Ashburn today.

I was born and raised in Ashburn when I was about to lose my home I went Colney Bank what was Ashburn Bank before Colney. Barbara Ann Perry was president of the bank my wife and mother borryed money from Barbara. She was thair lone officer when theay needed money theay went to her. Me and my dad had a business we barryed a lots of money from the bank and Barabara knew this. But doing those days she was not the president. I went to her she knew me and my family. None of us bored money from the bank and did not pay back.

I told here what I needed. She ask me what my creditor scores was I told her I don't know. How much do theay need to be and she said 600 and this as in 2008. And she said do you want me to run theim. I said sure. But I also know every time your scores are run, it takes some away from your scores. But she ran mine and mine was 597. She said Cleve I am sorry I can't help you. I said Barbara this is my home we are talking about. She sit thaire with her head down. I said Barbara I was born here Ashburn is home You are my last hope between me and my daughter being put out.

She said I am sorry I can't help you. I look straight at her she drop her head. I have not talk to her cence but I am not angry with her. I was when she would not look at me because I wanted her to remember how someone look when theay are about to be put out of thaire home.

I was talking with a banker about something about 2 years after I had lost my home and he ask how did I lose my home. I told him what happen and he said she could have let you have the money because your score proble was 600 and when she ran you score it knock off about 3 points cause every time you score it knock off about 3 points. I heard the old folks say you be treated better away from home theain you do at home.

Lesten I have good credit everywhere but where I grew up. I can't get a car financed here. I can by a car in Tifton. Thomasville, Albany, Macon, Leesburg and can't where I grew up that is a shame. You know when I need help I go out of town my daughter is the only thing that is keeping me here. Ashburn is no place for blacks. If you want to try and have something for your fiamley even I was born here. I know people was born here theay left here and doing much better. Ashburn is not the town it use to be. I would not invite nobody to come here and if you are black, you just asking for trouble. If you come here if I didn't live here I would not come here

We as a black race of people can do just what the whites do. All we asking is a chance. Obama wants to give everybody a chance and this is why we have a divided nation. Theay white don't want a black man telling them what to do. But theay have been telling a black man what to do for over 100 years. So I am sorry a black man will tell you and your children what to do before its over

You know I am an older man now but I did not think I would be writing a book about Ashburn. But most of all I did not know that we blacks are still hated by whites in 2013.

I got something I want to share with the readers. None of this should come as any great surprise. In 2010, the *New York Times* poll of tea partiers found more than half said policies of the Obama administration favor the poor and 25 percent thought that the administration favors blacks over whites compared with 11 percent of the general public.

Thaire racial paranoia has long been clear. If anything has been surprising its been potency of thaire hatred. Many I hope we are not hated blacks like this where I grew up listen to the irrationality of thaire tactics. The venom backlash but as theay see it theay are fighting or thaire way of life theay control. Thaire power. So you see readers this is what this shut down of the government is all about whites. Thaire control, thaire power and theay don't want a black man telling them whites what to do.

And he is the president of the United States the highest office. In the world and theay don't even respect him. Those kind of people should be ran out of the country and not allowed to come back. This is an insane battle and theay're willing to burn down the country to save it from people of color.

That's why theay willing to risk defaulting on the nation's debt for the first time in history. Man we are hated real bad. None of us cannot help what color we are. You mean to tell me we have people here at home feel like and hate like that. Don't look no further the terrorists are here. Theay just need locking up. I am proud of my color the Lord gave it to me and man can't take it from me. So after receiving what I received by e-mail I just don't know how to even be around people like that.

I mean all of us are human being why would anyone want to control any one because of skin color? Why would anyone want power over we are all in this together far as controlling nobody is going to control me

Moonshine and Living in the Deep South

or push me around. I don't know who the tea party think theay are but blacks we are not going to be did anything to but treated right. Or blood will be running in the street like water.

But you see all people of color are not stupid. So why don't we let the President do his job and we help him not try to tear him down. Because you don't know who the next president will be it might be another black man or woman or Mexican. So you have to be careful how you degrade people. You might just need those people and people don't forget statements what theay been listen at on radio and TV and in the paper.

Don't have anything to do with those N but after I got out of school in the 50's, and in the 70's the schools integrated and all the kids were going to school together. That is when the white kids found out that mommy and daddy were lying about us the black race. So now it is all out and you are losing control of your kids and everything that goes with it. You see we all were made by the same God. Everything he made was good and very good you see he did not make nothing

He made something you know when I began to write this book, my growing up in Ashburn, Southwest Georgia, I told about me being born here about my boyhood and teenager life and going to Eureka School , my marriage and the death of my wife and mother and father and so on. Little did I know that almost at the end of my book that our government would be shut down but it did so.

I am going to put it in my book for the small kids and the kids to come can read what kind of congress we had in 2013 and how theay disrespect the first black president the country has ever had. Hopeful when these young people come along it won't be groups like the tea parties trying to control thaire president who ever it might be. It is 2013 even our city and country are fighting over tax money everybody is fighting over money. The Bible say is it not a sin to have money. But the love of money that's when you get in trouble. Look at our country today October 16, 2013. People in offices are being paid off to wreck this country and it is not the president.

The young people of the future can read about it in my book. Because some of them is nothing but babies now. Theay will know what happened in October 2013. The country was shutdown. It is 11:30 p.m. I am sitting at my eating table writing this book. I have been blessed when I was young out thaire having fun I didn't think about getting old.

But you know what I thank the Lord I will be 76 this November 2. Lord I think you a lot of my classmates and friends has gone on home.

My two daughters I know theay love me very much and I love them too. My baby girl is still with me. She is a daddy baby but we get along just fine. She said Mr. Dye said you was fast when you ran track. I said I was and she said I bet you can't catch me. I laugh and said baby dad's old knees won't let him and said oho dad. I said baby these old knees have a lot of miles on them. She said dad can you still run I said yes and she said let me see. I took off making those short strides instead of long ones she just laugh.

I rode over by the housing project on Steven Street and just look and shut my eyes and think about how it was when and how it is now. Back then the streets was dirt, he lawn grass was pretty and green. Theay did not want you to walk on the grass. Theay had sign that said keep off grass. If you mother or dad seen you walk on the grass, got a whipping.

But now the streets are paved the yards is just as clean as my hand paper everywhere. It don't look nothing like it did when we lived thaire. You have a lot of young people live thaire who don't care. You have a lot of young men who those young ladies have for thaire live in boyfriend who sell drugs. And we have a police department who has an all white force. With about two blacks and about 11 or 12 whites and theay act like theay are afraid of those guys in the project.

I told one of the city council members theay need more black officers before theay see any results. Because those white officers are afraid. I seen those white officers on a call over on the west side theay call it. When theay drive up and get out of the car, theay start to cussing and calling names N with thaire hands on thaire gun. Then theay come back and say we can't get any help in the neighborhood. No you done went over thaire and cuss those people out and call them N names and think theay going to help you.

It is a pretty sunny day in Ashburn, South Georgia this 17th day of October 2013. I was just thinking one time we were at school Eureka and decided we was going to skip Mrs. King math class we went and hid in the football field house. And after the math class was over we sneaked back to our home room which was Mr. Dye. So later on we were let out for lunch and when we return to the class room Mr. Dye called all of us guys up and said Mr. King want to see you guys in his office. Then one of the guys said I wonder what Mr. King wants? I said man I don't know so we walked in his office and he said have a seat fellows.

Then he said why you fellows skip your math class? Before we could say anything he said don't lie because I seen everyone of you fellows.

Don't you know that you need math more than anything else. You guys think Fess is going to whip you but I'm not. What I want you fellows to do is on paper, I want you to write (I need math) 500 times before you go home and bring it to my office. If you leave and go home and I have to come and tell mom and dad you know what's going to happen.

But I never figured out how he knew we had looked before we went into the field house. But everyone went to Eureka can tell you how smart Mr. King was. But the only thing he was doing was getting us ready for today 2013. Look if you don't know math, you can't count money and people will rob you blind. I seen people who can't count money. I feel sorry for them.

I am going to talk a little more about growing up at a time when my father Jetty Brown and his friends out of Florida, Smith and Johnnie. I will never forget those guys even if theay were white, theay was just like family. Even back then, I never heard them use the N word. Theay were real men. Theay would sit down at our eating table and eat along with us. Then we would go down to the still, fire her up, and let her run. I can write about it now because all the people that was involved has passed away. You know those was the good old days. If people was like the people back then, things would be a lot better. Stay out of other people's business. That's the way it was back then.

That is why Smith, my dad did not get caught. People kept thaire mouth closed. But today in Ashburn. People are in everybody's business even the white people be asking what happened on the west side of town. But you have some people today if theay would have come along when the civil rights marches were going on and running thaire mouth. Theay would have got the hell beat out of them back in the 60's.

When the movement and SCLC as going on you did not talk to anybody about anything. I learned early not to talk about business with nobody who wasn't Johnny or Smith or my dad. You see that is why dad and the guys never got caught because people did not talk. You see the law don't know what you are doing at your house unless theay have Someone theay have paid to slip around and spy on you.

But my white brother up north are a little different from the brothers in the south. The Northern brothers will smile in your face and put a knife in your back. Look how theay do the president. But theay said one time he was not American. Then he was not black and now theay are saying theay don't want a black man telling them what to do. These are my northern white brothers.

But these Southern red necks will let you know but I think I can put up with my home boy's down here better than those sneaky Northerners. That's what I'm talking about. You bruise his head before he bruise your heel. I don't care what kind of cake you have it has to be cut. I am speaking from a black man's point of view. When you talking with a man you can pretty well know what kind of a man you are talking with. If he can't look you straight in the eyes when you talking with him, or he turn his head, he is bad news and another sign.

If you are talking with him on business. I'm talking about the good old boys in South Georgia. If he do either one of the two things I mention, then you know what to do. Leave him the hell alone. Because whatever you ask him to do he's not going to do it. I don't care what he tell me from then on, I'm not going to believe him because he has showed all the signs in my book that say no.

On One Friday me and my uncle was walking down Washington Street and he said Cleve do you want to drank a good cold one. I said yes. So we stop buy the Green Apple and walk up to the bar and sit down. And Leory Bell said can I help you boys? I said give me a Miller and James said give me a Bud. By that time, Leroy ask my uncle James to see his I.D. James pull out his ID and let him see it. And he said Cleve is about two month's older than me. Leroy said I know Cleve is old enough because we have drank and also know your mother James, Mrs. Mathis. And I said that's my grandmother and Leroy said I did not know that I said sister and brother and children.

I said give us another beer a piece and he said okay. I ask James did he want to shoot a game of pool. He said ok. So we did until these two girls came up, Shirley and Daisy, and started with them. Daisy was my girl and James like Shirley. So we hung out with them the rest of the day and it began to get dark and we had to walk them home. You see we did not have cars like the kids today. Everywhere we took our girls we had walk to the movie, ball games, prom, church. The kids of today just don't know theay got it made.

I just can't get away from Apt. 225 Stevens S housing project. It is too many memories to not write about we chase the girls at night. WE had cookouts. Ya'll we had cookouts back then we even got up du-bop group and we were pretty good. It was four of us. We wanted to be like the four tops. See back then you had a groups like the Drifters. Jackson five, and the O'Jays, the Platters, Jackie Wilson, the Midnighters, and Little Richard, Ben King, James Brown, Chuck Berry and we were trying to make

Moonshine and Living in the Deep South

it. Back then we did not know how to contact people like Barry Gordy or Motown.

We was in the deep South and first of all we did not have any money because we were still in school and our fathers was not like Joe Jackson. So I guess that is why we did not make it. WE did not have any money. Our parents did not have money for that because we had to live. So just quit singing and we got up a boxing team. It was about 10 or 15 of us guys. So we started boxing and I got knocked out by my good friend Jimmy Jordan. We call him Cotton Jack. That was the hardest I had ever been hit in my life. But it was fun and we enjoyed it nobody got mad. So what are you going to do? Get mad. You got the gloves on get mad and lose it and get whipped. Boxing is like any other sports when get mad that's when you don't care. That's when you are going to get whipped or give the game away.

Our legacy of Eureka elementary and High School was an outgrowth of the public elementary of Ashburn which made its appearance in the early thirties this school moved slowly for ten years are more than the class of 1941 was the first to graduate from the 11th grade with 10 units of work enabling its graduates to enter college.

In the early years of Eureka the following persons served as principal of the school Mr. H.L. Williams, Mr. G.P. McKenny, Mr. E.E. Owens and Mr. A.C. McKenzie. The homecoming activities that became a delightful part of our school days were started in the 40's in 1945. Our king, Mr. Hodge King became principal of Eureka School and remained in this position until the integration of the Turner county Schools County wide consolidation for high school students came in 1948 and the first bus for transportation was provided in 1949 Eureka made rapid progress in the 50's.

The first 12th grade class to graduate was in 1952. The football team was organized. This same year with Mr. John Dye as coach. The school had 21 teachers on its faculty. By 1953 an enrollment of 600 and four buses provided to transport students. The band was also formed in 1953 with Mr. Robert Cross as Director. At this time the school owned a 40 passenger bus for the purpose of transporting students on education tours and other trips connected with the school.

In the fall of 1957, the students of Eureka entered the new school building during this October 20 year. Eureka received its first free lunch program. The first yearbook printed for the school was the 1958 edition of the Tiger. Eureka continued to progress during the 60's. The school was also well known for its football, basketball and track activities. The last days of Eureka as we knew it were during the 1969-70 school year. By this time Eureka had 40 teachers on the faculty and 1000 students.

The school was renamed for the 1970-71 school year. Now I am asking a question. Why would want to take a school that is doing well with the name it has had for 40 or 50 years and change the name? Integration should not had anything to do with the name of the school. The blacks of Ashburn was not asked or told why the name was changed. Just like always the whites in Ashburn has done like theay wanted to do for so long till theay think it's right. And after theay took the name that was not enough theay kept on founding fault. Then theay started talking about closing the school.

So me and the President of the NAACP and some more members we went to have a talk with the superintendent of the schools. The excuse he gave us was the white teachers was afraid to teach over thaire. We asked him how can theay be afraid to teach over thaire when thaire kids be over thaire with the blacks every day after school. So that lie would not work so theay had to come up with another lie to get it to work. So theay came up with the ambesto contamination problem in the class rooms and it work.

I never heard about no one checking to see was that true. I did not read in the paper where the state checked it out. I think it was a ploy because theay wanted all the schools on the east side of town. But what theay didn't know or didn't care. Theay were destroying the legacy of a black school that was mostly built by the students. When you destroyed the Eureka School on Highway 112 West Washington, it was the same Eureka on South Jefferson Street but the black people of is not stupid. Theay knew what was going on. Eureka was moving too fast. We have over 1000 students. Probably more than Turner County High. So somebody had to come up with a plan to shut the school down and theay did.

But guess what God has a plan for all my white brothers that had a hand in closing our school. We know what happened and we know who had a hand in it. You will get paid for your wrong doing. Some have already got paid and some more are going to get paid. So when theay move to a new address and you don't see them anymore, you can just say theay are getting paid. I was told that alot of Eureka stuff was thrown away. Some was good and some was not. But someone could have called some of us we would have picked it up.

You can rest assured we the older students know who pushed for the school to be closed and everything. One day the truth will be told about the school and the land it was sitting on. Turner County and the City of Ashburn have took a lot of land from poor blacks. The young people don't know this but the older blacks know. The older whites are not going to say anything because theay might be guilty. The way the county and city are fussing over tax money that is some of the stuff happened when you treat your brothers wrong. You will pay the price.

When you do things unjustly, you have to pay for it. You might overcharge me in a store but that's ok. You will lose it. You might over charge me for things but that's okay. I will pay it. And when things start to happen to your business remember what goes around comes around. I can remember not long ago when I asked a friend of mine I thought for a favor and he turned me down. He did not do it. But that's fine. I made it. I'll be ok.

People the only true friend is Jesus.

You know Eureka our school was torn down after law agency used it for skating exercise. Theay would have never allowed them to do that in a white neighborhood. I have had people to ask me why ya'll keep worrying about Eureka and I ask them did theay attend the school and theay say no. It's only a school. Yes, you are right. A school we the students build and we loved the school. It was the only thing at that time that we had a hand in doing. We had a slogan in our 2010 reunion book that said you can tear down the building, but you can't take away the memories. That's I don't care what people say us older student that went to the old Eureka it was the real Eureka and we know this.

But in the 1970's the white got in the school. The first thing theay done was change the name of the school. The second thing theay done was to demote Mr. King from principal at the school for around 40 years. What happened is that the white people were so racist at that time and still is. Theay tried to turn Eureka white but theay knew theay could not do thaire dirty tricks in a black neighborhood so theay had to come up with a plan to get the school from over on the west side of town. And theay came up with one and theay pull it off. But I know Ashburn is one of the racist little town in South Georgia.

And some of the white people that move here from other places say I rember right here in Ashburn we use to have fairs come here. But we don't have them anymore. I rember theay would sit up on the spot across Hwy. 112 in front of the red barn. That was nothing but a large field at what is Tom Whitsett Park. All of them would be large fairs. Most times theay would have a Ferris wheels. And most of all what I liked back then was cotton candy, roasted peanuts, popcorn, orange soda. Back then kids 12 years old and older had to pay 25 cents at the gate to get in and grown- ups I think 50 or 70 cents to get in.

And man on Friday night, Saturday night you talking about the people man theay would be thaire. But you know what the police would be thaire but theay would not look up anybody unless theay was fighting or drunk and staggering all over everybody. I know a lot of people out thaire would be drinking because my dad would be. But he would not be drunk because he had to drive back home eight miles north of Ashburn to Sibley.

I was so glad when we moved to Ashburn in the project. Because a lot of us would walk up town and to the ball park when the fair come to town. We was never stop by the police. When I tell people theay say times a different now. I will quickly say no time is no different. People are because we had crime back then and we have crime now. We had mergers, burglaries, rapes, arson and everything. Thaire is no different. Just the people are. We have the same God now we had back then. I do.

After we moved from Ashburn to Sibley, shortly after we moved up thaire about two years later I had to start school. Back then blacks did not have school buses to haul them to school in Ashburn. So I had to go to school at our church in Sibley. My first teacher was Mrs. Odessa Clark, my second teacher was Mrs. Osie Lee West and I liked both of them. We had to walk about two miles one way to school. Sometime the rain would catch us before we could reach home. It was not bad in summer to get caught in a rain but in winter you would freeze.

I went my first year to school at New Hope Baptist church at Sibley. It stands today. It's almost one hundred years old. And the pastor of New Hope then was Reverend Leroy Adkins. He baptized me when I joined New Hope Baptist church. I moved my membership after we moved back to Ashburn. The pastor at New Hope today is Reverend Leroy's son, Reverend Joseph Adkins, but New Hope today is twice the size it was when we went to school thaire. I spent some cold days in that church in school you could feel the cold in it back then. We had those pot belly heaters that burned wood or coal and some time if we beat the teacher to school we would have to stand on the outside and wait until the teacher get thaire because the church would be locked. I would be so cold. Some mornings my hands and feet, kids just don't know.

I went to a gospel concert in Albany a few years ago and had a good time. It was on one Saturday night and we talked to some of the guys about coming over to Ashburn the next time theay come through. So sure enough the next time theay was down this way, we talk with them and theay book a program for that summer. Ok, when the time came theay came on down. I t was about six or seven groups so the program began at 6:00 p.m. in the afternoon.

We had groups from Illinois, New York, Ohio, South Carolina, Tennessee, Augusta, Atlanta when you have that many groups it takes a lot of time for them to perform and give the people something for thaire money. I guess it was about half through the programs lady was sitting by me. She said I wonder what is wrong. I said what you mean and she said two policemen just walked in.

I seen one of the men who was selling tickets at the door was talking to one of the policies. Theay said it is time for you all to go. It is 11:00 p.m. and you all have to leave. This was at the Civic Center here in Turner County. I was so ashamed. Our tax money hope build the center and we can't have a gospel concert. I never seen anything like that before. I have been to the Civic Center over in Albany till 2:00 o'clock in the morning. No police ever came in and said that. Some of the groups had never come back to this little racist Jim Crow town. Theay said theay have been all over the world singing and have never seen anything like this.

Someone had told Mary Frances office that when theay start to tear down the old school, theay would not tear down auditorium and kitchen because theay were in pretty good shape and it would not take much to fix it. But theay tore it down along with the rest of the school. That tell me just what theay say about the white man speak with forked tongue. That is true.

Look when I used to go to the movie here and see a cowboy and Indian movie, I though the Indian was the bad guys. But later as I got older, I found out the white man was trying to take thaire land like theay did ours. You know the white man has always took cheated all his life. He has never worked like the peoples of color. He has always wanted to be in control way back in the 17th and 18th century and it is 2013 and he still think he should be in charge to tell the people of color what to do.

But white brother it is a new day new time new people. You play the same a long time and played it well so it's time for you to get pay back for all you done to the poor people of color. All the land you from our ancestors and you are still trying to do it. Know when enough is enough. Brother you might as well get ready all your big fine houses and cars you bought with our land and money you stole. You have never got anything honest you has always worked the people of color for nothing.

Life because some of them did not know any better. Don't you know you can do wrong for so long now. You are saying you would rather see the country burn than see it run by a people of color. You took everything from the people. It was not supposed to be like this. But you broke all God's laws. Thou shalt not steal, thou shalt not kill, and thou shall not bear false witness. You have broken almost every law in the Bible and think you are going to get away with it. No. You have to pay here on earth and when you meet God so if I was you I would start right now trying to undo what I have done wrong.

My white brother we the people of color has never done you no wrong. But you have enslaved us you have lynched us. You have raped our women, you burn us to death. Our mothers have raised and looked after you children, cleaned your nasty house, cooked your meals. Don't you think it is about time you do something for yourself. Or you afraid that your kids will found out what kind of dad theay have. He got everything he got from his dad. Cheated, stole killed for it took it from people of color that's why we are poor.

We have never recovered from what was taken from us. I was in a store. I heard a white' man talking. He said I worked hard for what I got. Theay don't want thaire kids to know that the land he owned has blood on it. But one day the truth will come out and it won't be long before the kids and everyone else know how he got it.

I was sitting here thinking how we the people of color, black, has been passed over and put back on everything such as jobs. Per motions we always are under paid. We always are given the dirty jobs and some one standing over you like you are in prison right thaire in Ashburn. People are not stupid. I work here in Ashburn where I thought I could make good money. But it turned out to be the cheapest job I ever work on. The money I was paid per hour I made that in the 80's and 90's here.

Where I grew up has not changed pay wise. You don't get paid for what you know. You get paid for what color you are. This is 2013 and people in these small towns in the South are still looking at color. Look I work on a job here theay started me at minimum wage $7.25. I work thaire six years so when I left I was making $8.13 per hour. It took me five years to make a 90 cent pay raise, but my white brother started working thaire a little before I left and he did not know anything, but guess what. Theay started him off with $9.00 per hour. Do you think that's right? No, that is not right.

When we were out of school, we would work in watermelons. Black and white boys work together. We were paid the same. The problem we have now some whites want everything to go backwards, but that will never happen.

I am a writer and I write for our newspaper here. So the other day, we were sitting out under verander talking and I had a newspaper and a friend of mine, who is white lady, she asked me if she could look at the paper and I said yes. And I asked her did she ever read my article. She said no. Because theay said you are a racist. Then I asked her what theay said that. Then she replied I would rather not say. Then I asked her what do you think? She said I don't think you are.

Well, I am not a racist, but whoever told you that probably is racist. Then I asked her why the lady said that about me. And she told me the lady said she had read some of my articles. I said well. I hope she enjoyed them. Because one thing about me I will write the truth so if it sounds racist to you I, I am sorry. I write it like I see it. If I go to a scene and see something I need to let my readers know about. I am going to write it just like I see and hear it. So if you a racist or name caller keep it to yourself. But anybody with respect for themselves will not use that nigger word in the first place. But we have mean and dangerous people in this world.

You know I can relate to growing up in the deep south in Ashburn and Turner county. Me and my cousins walking up town on Washington Street back then it was a two lane highway. We would walk passed the oil mill and would smell the peanut oil. It smelled like peanut butter. But today it is golden peanut mill. But that oil smell would make you so hungry. I used to love to walk by just to smell it. Where the red barn is today was a small store. It was run by a little old white lady named Mrs. Grayer. She sold hot dogs and everything. On 112 Highway was so narrow two cars could just pass one another. Some people would just walk up town and sit and talk. Some of the stores windows was built you could sit in them. People would stand on the streets and talk. Sometime the police would walk up and join in. You back then we had friendly officers. Theay knew almost everyone in Ashburn. Theay would not walk and say where are you going. What you got your hands in your pockets for. We did not hear any of that back then.

And this was in the 50's and early 60's. You could walk the streets here day and night and not be stopped by the police. Ashburn had crime back then like it had today. We had to walk everywhere we went. We did not have cars like the kids today. Our parents could not buy us cars like the parents of today. But we were not going to jail like the kids of today either. In some ways Ashburn was better back in the day than it is today in some ways. But nobody's going back in those days. Theay are gone bye bye.

I told you not to mess with that gun and disobeyed what I said now. Pull it off I am going to whipt you. I am going to learn you to do what I say. Mother said jetty don't whip him this time. Dad said Arlean that's the trouble now you let Cleveland get by. I am going to whip his (A) and yours to if you don't get out of the way. Boy that long tall black man put something on me. Man I did not have on anything back then that is the way most black boys were chastised. Back then if the Judge would have got in the way, he would have got hit. Back then people raise thaire children.

The white man came up with a law call child abuse. The reason I said white man because no blacks pass anything. Look the highest court in the land Supreme Court theay only have one black on the bench. He can't stop anything and he can't pass anything. So you see this abuse thing is to keep you from whipping your kids where theay the white man's court can put them in the system. Because kids will be bad and do anything if theay are not chastised. But when my dad turned me loose, I did not touch that gun again. A parent is not going to kill thaire children. Shotgun in my closet today every time I pick it up, I just rub my back end and thank my dad for raising.

If you were black and poor living in Ashburn in the 50's, it was hard, but our parents made it because back then you could find a job anywhere. You had Scotts Saw Mill. You had Scott's chicken farm. You had Ashburn Peanut Company. You had William's Peanut Mill. And a lot more jobs. I never heard anyone say that the people would not work like I hear today. I think what it is the people what are saying theay want work are not being truthful about the whole thing. I think what it is theay want work for what theay want to pay them. People will work if you pay them. You can no longer make it on $7.25 per hour when things in the stores are going up every day. People should be ashamed to ask or offer people $7.25 per hour when things in the stores are going up every day. And people should be ashamed to offer people $7.25 per hour to work.

You don't hear that nowhere but where I grew up. In other places like Tifton, Cordele, Sylvester and other places, theay start you off at $8.88 per hour. People know what the minimum wage is but you can't live off it so why keep offering it. Special the young people and I don't blame them. You see you get what you pay for. Nothing from nothing. Leave nothing and cheap from cheap leaves poor. So when you say people want work just remember you are paying them nothing for all that work you want them to do. Put yourself in thaire place with a wife and family, kids to go to school house rent. What could you do with $7.25 per hour, nothing.

I look back over my growing up here some of my friends I grew up with are gone, but God blessed me to still be here and I thank him. I know that I am not the best person in the world and I am not the baddest one either. But I try to treat my fellowman right, but some time people will take your kindness for your weakness. I was taught to speak to people even though some of them won't speak but I leave them in the hands of the Lord. Here in Ashburn I know who is keeping me alive and that is the only true friend you can have, Jesus Christ. So I don't worry about what man say anyway.

You know when I was young growing up in the housing project, I never thought about getting old that never crossed my mind. I was talking to a good friend of mine, Tom Whitsett the other day. I said, man where did the time go? He said Cleve, the time flew. He said man, it seems like yesterday. We were running track together. I said, man both of us are in our 70's. But health wise, we both are in pretty good shape. I can't forget my Uncle James Mathis he is my mother's baby brother. He is the only one left out of nine children. Me and him, my cousin, Sam Hampton, who passed away a few years ago grew up here in Ashburn. We were just like brothers.

I was sitting on my car thinking way back about how a man named Mr. Tom White used to sweep the street of Ashburn with a push broom. He would all ways wait till midnight when the people leave and go home.

I also remember when we did not have but a garbage trucks for the City of Ashburn. I know theay had two hard working black men. Mr. George Wilson and Mr. Bobby Key Gamble. And back then we had 55 gallons can for garbage cans back then. The trucks were two ton trucks. And theay had low sides but the trucks a little high from the ground. Theay had to pick those 55 gallon drums up and dump the over the side of the truck. And that was hard work for two men. Back then you did not see too many white men working for the city unless he was driving something. A lot of those guys working for the city now would have not made it. But thaire is nothing change with the city now. The black men are still doing all the hard work and maybe one or two whites. But the rest are riding around in new trucks. Theay don't need and you one setting in a truck watching two or three men working what a waste of tax money.

You know growing up in the south the early 60's for blacks when you were a teenager was no piece of cake. Back then it was yes or and yes mam. But some of the older people miss and Mr. John Doe but to me I would say yes. No mother and dad would say boy you better say yes sir and yes mam to Mr. John Doe. And when Mrs. Mary bring you home you better get in the back seat of that car. But I did not I got in the front seat with the lady. She did not tell me to get in the back seat. She just smiled. I never had any trouble back then.

I think the older people back then was more afraid than the young people. What would make me mad when you went to Smith Café up town you would have to go in the back alley and get your food out of a window. You go to a water foundation it would have one with white only and one with colored. I always said that's crazy. No one is going to put thaire mouth on it anyway.

But that was in the Jim Crow days. Things have changed but not a hell of a lot because just like back then, we were under payed then and we are still underpaid. I don't get it. If I can do the job, pay me what the job called for. Color has nothing to do with the job getting done. The Jim crow days was hung up on color and now in 2013, the rednecks are still trying to underpay thaire black brother. I thought this late in time the paying game what theay have been paying for years would be over by now but it's not.

Well I guess we are going to run some more moonshine. Smith and dad are ready. So I guess I will fire it up. Theay are getting the jugs of the wagon and the corn is ready. You know this was fun for me. Back then because I don't think another kid in Turner experienced what I did. And I think theay would have been afraid. But by me being the only kid dad and mom had I got to do a lot of things. Other kids would only dream of.

But it was something I am glad I done and now I can speak out about it and no one get hurt or go to jail. But back then my lips were sealed. Back then I got anything and everything I wanted. But back then my dad would not put money in the banks in Ashburn because he knew the people in Ashburn would be asking questions like theay always do.

If a black man put a large sum of money in the bank, theay even do that today. So what dad done was put money in the bank's out of town like Albany, Tifton and Cordele where people did not try to get in your business like theay still do in Ashburn. One thing about a small town like Ashburn you cannot let nobody know what you are doing. If Ashburn would have known what dad and Smith and Johnnie was doing, the feds would had got them by the time we set the still up. And some people still talk too much in Ashburn. But you have those Uncle Tom's that tell the white man everything the blacks do, but back then we would have beat the hell out of him. Ok.

I would like to talk about a man who became a legend in his own time. That man is Mr. Hodge King who was my second dad, my teacher, my friend and my principal. Mr. King will always be remembered by all of his students. He will be remembered for his leadership in the schools in Turner County. He is missed bad in the black neighborhood and so is his late wife Mrs. King. Both of these two people did a lot in Ashburn and a lot for the kids in Ashburn. He educated about three generations of kids. Mr. King will long be remembered for his contribution to education in Turner County.

We use to ask him was he kin to Martin L. King. He would smile and say no, but we heard he was, but we did not know for sure. Mr. King was born November 10, 1914 in Dooling, Georgia. Mr. King prepared for his career at three educational institutions. First, Morris Brown College he received a Bachelor of Arts degree. He obtained his Masters degree from New York University. At Atlanta University, he obtained his six year certificate in educational administration. Over the years Mr. King received countless awards. Some of the awards and recognitions he received were the Turner County Chamber of Commerce Citizen of the Year in 1985, Silver Beaver Award from the Boy Scouts in 1986, Principal's award for merit for outstanding service in 1970, and the Morris Brown College National Alumni Association Purple and Black Service Award.

Mr. King and us his students what you might say built Eureka School. That's why we loved that school. Anything that you have something in you love it and that is why we talk about it. Mr. King came to work in Turner County in 1948. Army barracks was obtained from Fort Benning, Georgia to provide space for a growing school. Mr. King's male students which was us helped to reassemble the barracks when theay arrived. We also assembled the seats the desks and we done a lot more to those barracks.

Where Ms. Ezell live today on South Jefferson her home was part of Eureka. It had six class rooms. It had a hall. Thaire was three rooms on each side of the hall. At the back on the left side we built a room for a snack shop. It sold cookies, candy, drinks and so forth. But most everything was from 5 cents to 10, 25 cents.

Man you could take a dollar. It would last all week. The smaller building between the Ezell house and where Mr. King lived which is now Barbara Pickett house as the library not the Ezell house. In the back we had a basketball court made of red clay that's where we had our basketball games. And when Coach Dye come on the scene, that's when football began in 1953. He organized the first football team. That's when the Tiger was born. The Eureka Tigers all the way. It will always stay.

I would like to talk about another man that became a legend in his own time. Mr. John Wesley Dye was born March 21, 1927 in Lake City, Florida. He is a graduate of Brooks County School in Quitman, Georgia and a graduate of For Valley State College, Fort Valley, Georgia. He has done further studies at Albany State College, Valdosta State and Atlanta University. Turner County provided him with his first and only job at Eureka High and Elementary school on Lee Street in 1957.

A new school was built. He was successful and won two state championships 1965 and 1966. Both victories over Boggs Acadamy in football, Sixth District Championship in basketball and many awards in track and field. He coached all sports at Eureka and was affectionately known as "chief." After integration, he joined the staff at TCHS in 1969 and had a very big hand in Turner County's first championship football team. In 1976, and two regional championships.

He was teacher of the year at Eureka in 1962 and at TCHS in 1970 and 1972. Chief is a good man. When I was in school he hope me a lots. He is just like a second dad. He is also my friend and was teacher. I knew him and Mrs. Dye before theay married me. Tom Henry and more guys ran track at Fort Valley State College when Mrs. Dye was in school at Fort Valley State. Chief taken us to see her when we were up thaire at a track field's day. We ran that day and won. We had some fun.

Hey what makes the world go around. Jetty Brown's moonshine. That's what the people use to say about my dad. Who has the best shine in town down town Brown. You know I was a small boy 12 or 14. Give or take my dad and his two friends Smith and Ralph. I will never forget those days on the farm. I learned a lot from those three guys.

I will never forget coming down to Christmas dad would always fix five gallons of whiskey for his buyers. We would come from Sibley to downtown Ashburn on Saturdays to get groceries from Mr. Lee Morrison's Grocery Store. And when my mother would order grocery, he would tell her, Arlean don't forget the dried peaches.

You know my mother would take them things and make what she would call peach puff. She would take them and put them in water and boil them and when she got through with them man, theay was good. But my dad would take some of them and put them in moonshine. He said that would give the moonshine a good taste and he would give each buyer a quart for Christmas. Some time he would have a Christmas dinner for them.

People need to stop this thing about racism. Even back In time, the race was mixing. Because theay used to come up to my dad's, white women would be with black men. Black women's with white men's back then. Theay were not in the public with it. But it was going on. So it's nothing new to me. Because I seen it way back then. I thought it was Ok.

You know back then we had more in a way we had our own meat. We could kill a hog or cow when we wanted to, but now you can't. You cannot raise your own meat you have to buy it. I don't see anything wrong with raising your own meat. We have the same government now we had back then. I think it is a state thing. So you will have to buy your meat and everything out of the stores.

In the fall of the year, we had a lot of pecan trees in our yard and the man, Mr. Williams, what my dad was farming with would let us pick them up on half where we could have money for Christmas. I know we would pick up a lot would not go and sell them until we had about a ton and he would sell them some time a ton would bring $500.00 back then that was a lot of money. Dad's part would come to $250.00. Man, when Christmas come we would have everything we needed and more. But now it ain't no way a farmer now would give the man what work for him. Him and his family half of the pecans that theay pick up. That's the difference now. Back then the people cared about thaire help. But nowadays theay don't.

Well you see all the good people are gone what we have now is cheaters. Blood suckers. Theay want to live off people like me and you. Ok. Like today in times. May 19, 2014, minimum wage $7.25 per hour. What will it buy, nothing. Meat in the grocery stores 4, 5, 6 dollars a pound versus $7.25 an hour. So you see what I am saying.

Poor people will always be poor unless theay stand up where the people cannot walk on them. I will tell you one thing about Cleveland Brown. I was raised up to give all people older than mere respect. It don't make any different what color theay was but the kids don't care anymore.

I can remember when you could buy cold drinks for 5 cents honey bun for 15 cents. That has not been one hundred years ago, but it's been a while. You know I look at Ashburn today and look at it from yesterday. It has not changed one hundred percent like it should have. It's sad to say we have people in Ashburn right today don't want change. But theay want change of prices in the stores.

No change in prices for employment. But I still say the government should not have force to race of children to go to school together because ever since that has happened our kids has failed in learning. A lot of people that don't know any better think it's the kids. Its not, it's the teacher. Why? Because first of all a white teacher cannot teach black kids because some teachers don't like black kids and the next thing theay don't want us to learn anything any way. Theay want us today to be just like our people was in the 1800's.

You know we have our brothers out thaire today trying to make a living but look like its harder now to get a job than it was in the 60's. I wonder what would people do if theay had to go through what went through in the 50's and 60's. We had to walk. Our parents was not able to buy us cars like the parents buy the kids of today. Theay did not make enough money making 50 cents to 75 cents per hour.

Let me just share something with y'all, you know you never forget your upbringing. Most of us brought up in the 50's have respect for older people. No matter what color theay are. We were raised like that. In my upbringing, my dad and mom taught me well. Theay told me that don't bother things don't belong to you. Always treat people like you want them to treat you. Be kind and nice but don't let them walk on you. Always greet people with a smile. Even if theay don't like you.

I had a chance to see this back in the 50's, 60's, 70's and 80's and even in the 90's. I have said this more than a dozen times, in this book it is sad that people (not my people) that other people let a little skin color keep a race of people divided. It is sad. Nobody is better than anybody. Because God made us all. Am I right? Unless somebody else made you. I know God made me. It is just as racist now. In 2014 as It was in 1914, don't be fooled by those quick smiles and short answers. We as blacks still is not liked in the south. It is so sad. People could hate a race of people for so long.

Now some time I hate I was born in this country. But its not the country, it's the people. But God has a plan for all of these wrong doers. I am just going to sit back and look at the change that's coming. It won't be long. All we have to do is sit back and look at God work. Now when we fix something it is fixed. So all of you people out thaire that's been stepping on us small people, you can look out. Payday is here. So you can pay your dues. You have had it good long enough. It's time for somebody else to ride the train of enjoyment and happiness. You people have had it good for the last 300 years. Y'all can rest.

I am about to tell you about my upbringing on the Williams Farm. We had a lot of things to be done on the farm. So while mother was cooking supper one evening, Cleve I said yes mam. You here that hen clucking? She has some baby chick's somewhere and I want you to find them. Ok, I started to looking for the hen nest. You see a lot of young people don't know what a hen net is. It is where the hen lay her eggs.

So I kept looking, but it's one thing mother did not tell me. That when I found it, do not bother or pick up any of the baby chicks. But it did not take very long to found out because when I found the nest I was down on the knees playing with the small baby chicks when here come mommy hen. Boy she jumped and tried to peck me in the face. I started running and crying. Mother came out the door with the stick broom and ran the hen away. I found out early in life everything will try protect thaire own.

I had a lot of work to do on the farm after school. Back then it was fun living on the farm. But you know its 2013 and 2014 here when I grew up. I bet we don't have a half dozen of black farmers. In Turner County and when I came up on the farm, thaire was a lot of black farmer's some as renting land and some owned thaire own farm. And theay was making a good living for thaire family and every one as doing well. But somewhere things begin to go wrong for the renter and the small land owner farms. But just like anything else the big fish eat up the small fish. Theay know how to put the small man out of business, raise the prices on everything and that will do it. So when that happen, the small landowner had to try and sell his little farm, but could not so he had to take anything to get rid of it.

I was sitting down one day and it came to me to write this book. I said I don't know. So I mention to my youngest daughter and she said write a book about what I said about my life on the farm and growing up here in Ashburn. She smiled and said go for it. Now this book might not be what you want to read about but everything in here is true because I am the one who done those things. I am the one things happen to. Thaire has been no names changes.

I begin writing this book at the age of 75 years old. I as then and still is in my right mind. If I misspell some words, take it for love. You know I should have started writing this book ten years ago. But I could not had put the stuff in here what has happened in the 2000 century and man it's a ton of stuff. We have had a lot of stuff happen here where I grew up to write a book about and maybe two books.

I just look and think if the people that built Ashburn could come back from the grave. People like the Shingler, Baldwin, Turner, Story, Ewing, Gilmore, Murray, Davis, Johnson, Evans, Harden, Kennedy, Thrasher, Betts, McKenzie. These are just some of the people that mostly built Ashburn. We built you and look at you now. You was not maintained and not kept up. Now look at you. You know money and greed is why Ashburn is in the shape it's in today. The people that owned those buildings on 41 north and south Main Street would rather see those buildings sit and rot than to rent them when theay was able to rent at an affordable price. What a waste.

I just sit back and listen. You know when I came up on the farm, we had to what you call shake peanuts by hand. That mean shake all the dirt off of them. We had to pick cotton by hand. Even back then, the Mexican would come to the U.S.A. and shake peanuts and pick cotton. But when all of this was over, theay would go back to Mexico. None did not try to stay in this country back then.

I am glad in my lifetime I got a chance to see this country with a black president all of us blacks on a few whites that are happy but then you have about 95 percent of whites hate the president. Including the congress and senate. White people in the Southern states don't like the president at all You know in the South, people say theay don't need a black man telling them what to do. I say get ready a black is going to be telling you what to do sooner than you think.

And if you living you will be working for us just like we once worked for them. So don't worry, your children will be working for us just like our kids work for you. But one thing about the Bible, it don't lie so get ready for payback. Theay say payback is hell, but somebody has got to pay for the wrong has been done to us.

I am so glad that we are getting something at the Old Eureka School Campus. We are getting a 56 unit apartment complex. Will be built on the Eureka site in West Ashburn. The apartments will be named after the school Eureka Heights Apartments. What a blessing. I told them when theay the blue eyes devils found a way to destroy our school that God will take care of his own. He always has so look what we got for them destroying our school in West Ashburn #1. A fire station #2, EMS Station #3, a new water tank the color Eureka School #4 solar panels.

And the people in West Ashburn has one man to thank for all of this, now the mayor or Ashburn, Mr. Jim Hedges, a man who was looking him and his Joan for a small place to live. Theay pull Ashburn up on the internet and theay pick Ashburn. Jim had already retired and about one year later he became Mayor of Ashburn. At that time he was the best thing that could happen to our small town. But we had mayors before Mr. Hedges but you know what I think, theay just did not give a damn. It took a man that did not know anything about Ashburn to come here and right off he seen what we black people needed. And he began to work on it.

He became Mayor and other mayors before Mr. Hedges did a lot to talk and that was all. But in this book that I am writing Mayor Jim Hedges will go down in the history of Ashburn for making a difference in West Ashburn. And all the black people know who did it. And we will always be grateful. Thank you Mayor Hedges.

I am going to ask you a question. You know our country has a double standard don't you? You didn't know that? Okay, I am going to show you. Okay, when my dad and Smith and Ralph was running moonshine, the law was bad. But not like theay are in the 2000 century. Do you know why theay was not like that back then? Because theay cared about people. It made no difference color you was. Theay cared and would try to help you if theay would drive up on someone staggering from too much to drink and knowed you and knew who you work for. Theay would take you home.

I was talking with one of my white guy friends and he said Cleve, I bet you know my dad. I said what's your dad's name. He told me, I said yes I know your dad. He said I bet I bet your dad have drank some of my dad's moonshine because he used to make it. I said no, but he has bought some moonshine from your dad and sold him some too. Because we had our own still back then. If theay caught you with moonshine. If you work for a man that had a lot of money, he would be thaire before theay lock you up. But now I know a black boy in prison now for having sex with a girl under 16. Okay, a white boy did the same thing. Only he did it twice but guess what the judge gave him, 10 years probation, but gave the black boy 20 years in prison. I call that is double standard. That happened right here in Ashburn. But if he had been my son, no way in hell I would have let that happen and not do nothing about it. I would be in Atlanta now.

I was born and raised here in Ashburn, but I thought it would be better you know. If I was a younger man, I would take a chance on running some moonshine. But I am too old to do it by myself and anyway the people are too scared of the law. And theay talk too much. You know we have some black folks will tell everything theay know. But like I always was told, keep peoples out of your business. When you are going to do something, don't tell anybody. My dad did not.

What I am telling now, would not be told if any of the people that was involved was alive. You know why I was taught that way. I know today people my dad did business with in Ashburn. Theay might not know me but I know them. And no one will ever know if I have to tell them. You see back then everybody involved in moonshine looked out for each other. If one moonshiner heard anything about the law, was planning a raid theay would let all the moonshiners know.

I remember one time the law bust my uncle's house. He was keeping some of dad's moonshine over at his house in an empty room. Theay poured out around 100 gallons of moonshine. It would take us about three or four days to run that. So you see that sit us back. We lost a lot of money back then. Five gallons would sell for $25.00. You talking about $500 back then five hundred dollars was like five thousand. So you know we was hurt more than one way. If you figure out labor and time we was hurt. Bad but we overcame it.

That was the first and last time we lost that much at one time you know. If you in any kind of business, you will lose sometime that's business. So what do you do? Suck it up and move on because if you stay in business, you will make it back.

If anyone reading this ever been in the moonshine business know what I mean, my dad Jetty Brown is the only man I know of with a 3rd grade education that you could not out count him counting money he could count it in his head while you are trying to figure it without a pencil. I never seen a man like him. The only time I seen him write his name was when he would go to the bank for a loan. Then he would write his name. Then it would look like chicken scratch, but you could read it.

My dad was a hell of a man but a good man. I know he told me one day me and him was riding along in the truck and he told me he said always treat people right son. Treat them the way you would want the to treat you and you will be doing the right thing. If you do this, you should not have trouble with your fellow man.

But by chance you do, always rember what I am telling you. Walk away from that person. Don't have anything to do with him because soon or later you will have trouble with him. I try to do what my dad taught me. And he always rember what I am telling you. And he also said no matter what color they are. And if theay get out of line you know what to do, beat the hell out of him. But make sure you are in the right.

I rember when I was growing up, my mother told me to go to the well. Some of the older people out thaire know what a well with a rope with a bucket on the end. That what you call a well. When mother would milk the cow, she would take the milk and tie it the bucket and let it down in the well. The water was cool enough to keep the milk from spoiling. And that's what she had told me to go and draw up and bring it to the house where we could have it for supper.

But I was playing and forgot to go and get the milk. So when dad came in from the field, he put the mules in the lot and I hope him feed them. We gave them hay and corn that's what dad fed them when he was working them. So mother called us to come on supper was ready. So we sit down to the table and dad blessed the food. And he said Arlean where is the milk in the ice box? She said no. I ask that young earley to go to the well and get it, but he kep playin.

Dad said I will take care of that. And he did that night when I went to bed. I was almost asleep. I felt the cover was being pull off of me. It was my dad with his belt. I did not have on anything but a night shirt. Man he whip the stew out of me. I bet I did not forget the next time, but you know back then your mother would not beg you to do something. She would ask you to and if you did not do it, when your dad get in from the field, she would tell him and that was it. Your father did not want to here anything you had to say. If you would try and tell him he would say are you calling your mother a lie.

I learned early not to question what she told my dad. But you know back when our parents was giving us all those whipping we thought theay did not love us, but theay did. I thank my parent for every whipping theay gave. It taught me to be a better man and how to treat people. And how to leave that alone that don't belong to me. It also leare me how to not do things that would hurt me or my fellow man. You know we have so many people out thaire today that don't have no regards for me or you or eather them self. You know theay should have came along when I did theay would rember it.

I cannot understand Ashburn older white people and young one's that has been taught thair parent and grand parent that theay are to work people for nothing. I am old, but I know you have to pay people a decent salary for them to live. I have grandchildren. I would not teach them to try and under pay people that work for them. But theay do that here in Ashburn. That is why Ashburn is like it is today.

If a company wants to come here and theay are paying the people good money, theay will found a way to stop it. I had a white friend that live here and ran a business here. He told me Cleve you black people need to wake up. I said what do you mean? He said every time you see those white people to those churches theay are not serving God. Theay are having meetings about you all. And I said for real, and he say yes. And you did not get this from me. I said ok. This was in the last of the 70's or early 80's.

So I told someone the blacks here in town and we started watching it and we found out through a reliable source it was true. But the same thing is happen today. You know most white people think black people are stupid. But we are not. We just are a race of people you cannot figure out. We are not like our race of people that y'all had ensaved way back. That will never happen again. So don't even try that. Because blood will be running like water.

Myself and my people or not stupid. We know what's going on. We are just sitting back looking and waiting on y'all little game to play out. Then y'all will see how stupid we are. Ok, God has a plan for all of us. You have to do is trust and obay. That's something the people of this town Ashburn have a problem with obaying our maker God.

I was just sitting here about the people of today and how theay are different from the people of yesterday and theay are not as smart. Because if theay were theay could see why no big companies want locate here. I think theay know and just too shamed to say so. Theay want locate here because we don't have a hospital. And we don't have good schools. And good hoseing for thair workers. And the race relation is not too good. And no recreation at all in town not even a movie.

So companys looks at all of that but you know what times were better here in the 60's and 70's and even better in the 80's. Now its 2014 and look like the town is going down. But like I said early maybe Wal-Mart will help pick it up. You some of the guys I went to Eureka School with when theay come back here theay say man what has happen to Ashburn Cleve? I say man I don't know. I try to explain but really I don't know.

For one thing the town is devided. If you think I am lying go to West Ashburn where its about 95 percent black and look how the streets are

Moonshine and Living in the Deep South

being keep up. And the ditch's maintain and then go to the east side witch is about 97 percent white and tell me what you see. Ok, you have taxpayers in West Ashburn and tax payers in East Ashburn. Ok, now you have seen both sides of town. Now tell me who are getting thair money's worth for thair tax dollar.

You don't know? The east side. Look at thaire streets. Theay done have holds in the road. Thair ditches have been dug out so when the water runs off the road in the ditch and not down the road this is what's wrong with Ashburn.

I love to talk about me being raised up in the deep South. Me and some of the older guys that's retired like myself. We hang out at a BP Service Station that is right off I-75 highway. So we get a chance to talk with a lot of people from up North. Theay be asking us about a lot of stuff about the South and what theay read about down here. And was it true and we told them it was.

One day ask me did theay still hang black people down here? I told her not any more. And she ask me do theay still use the N word down here and I told her people do and some don't. Man she and I guss that was her husband with her man theay talk with us about an hour. Theay was say that we did not deserved to be treated like we have been for the last hundred years and I agreed with her.

But I told theam it was better but we still have some racist right here in Ashburn and some KKK. But theay think we black's don't know but we know. And don't care because we are not afread of them. But you know I don't think the South will ever get like it need to be. It has change some but thaire is still room for improvement but you know we still has some with that Jim Crow and slavery mentality. And we have some of the older ones. You can tell theay still hate black's today.

How can people that God created live with hate in them when God is all about love? I have seen some people I don't like thaire ways but as a person I do not hate any one. I know our white brothers have done us wrong all our lives, but I do not hate them, I love them.

I was sitting down talking with my daughter last night and she said do you rember when granddaddy use to tie my boot's up every morning when I was getting ready for school? Yes I had forgot it and she made me rember it. I am so glad she was about five or six years old and my dad bought her pair of black boots and every morning when her mother get her ready for school, she would go up to granddads and he would tie her boots for her. I would keep them shine for her but she would not let me tie them up.

And when my dad past away, I will never forget the look on her face when she came in the room and seen him. She ask her mother, my life what was wrong with granddaddy. Her mother told her granddaddy was asleep. And she ask was granddady going to tie her boots when he wake up. That's when I step in and tried to explane that to a seven year old kid.

I told her the best I could at that time. But as time went by she understood as much as a seven year old could right after we buried my dad. She told me daddy you will have to tie my boot's for me because ganddaddy is not going to wake up. When she told me that I almost broke down in tears but I rember what my dad once told me. No matter what happened, a man is supposed to stand up and be strong no matter what the case is. But its real hard when you have lost your father and you have to explane it to your seven year old little girl about her granddad.

I tell all the young people if theay don't know Jesus Christ who is the head of all our lives what are they living for. You know I think the Lord every day for keeping me.

I hope everybody that read my book read this. Every since we had a black president, I don't know how it is up north but in most of your southern states, you read and here on the news we are gonna take our country back. You here a lot of that down here. Look nobody has took no country. The country has not gone anywhere. What is wrong with people in the two thousand century?

Nobody can take God's country. I know we as a black race of people know that we don't own it. But I think you would have a hard time convincing the southern white people that. Because theay really think theay own it. We as a black race of people don't own anything, but that are wrong because we fought in the civil ware just like theay did more than 38,000 negro soldiers lost thair lives in the civil war. It has been estimated that their rate of mortality was nearly 40 percent greater than that among white troops. So theay are not the only one that has something in this country. Over 186,000 blacks fought under the union flag during the civil war. But you have a lot of white people running around thinking theay own this country.

I guss theay are going to take God's creations. But not so because man has already messed it up so bad that he don't know what to do. What man who you think the white man. WE the black man has never had any authority in this country since he was free from slavery in the south or north. I have never read anywhere in history where a black man or woman even helped write or sign anything in this country into law.

I'm sitting over here where I work during the summer. It's a splash pad to the kids playing in the water. Black and white kids are playing togeather. Just like Dr. King said so. You see if the kids can play togeather, why we grownups can't get along. I can tell you why. Because the white man in the south still have that old slavery mentality to talk to a black man any kind of way.

And that's not going to work in 2014 so theay can forget that. I would like to see all of us down here but the people in the south have been wrong so long theay its right. I myself as a black man was raised in the south I was born here. It is some better but it could be better if the white mails would treat black men like men and not boys. But don't look like theay don't want change but change is coming. I never understood how one grown man think he can be the ruler over other mens'.

I use to here my grandmother say her mother would be talking about slavery how the masters would beat and kill the black men's and rape the black woman and nobody did anything about it. She said theay would feed the slaves like hogs. I have read it in the books at the bookstore. I ask my daughter did theay teach black history when she was in school? She said yes. But it was nothing like this. I said I know because theay did not want thaire children to know what thaire grate, grate grandparnat done back then but theay will found it out sooner or later. That's why I try to not do things that will ruin the family's name.

I can't forget my early life that I grew up on the farm. I will never forget something I had to help do on the farm. I had to help mother chop cotton. Some people don't know what that is. I am going to try and tell you what that is.

Ok. Back then the farmer would plant the cotton thick just like theay do today. Then he would get a crew of people to take hoe's what we use to clean our flower beds with and let them chop or hoe the cotton out and leave about four of stalk's to the hill. But years later the farmer found out theat he was chopping up his profit so they stopped doing that.

But we had to pull corn by hand and pick soil beans by hand. But you know what farmed life back then was more better for poor blacks and white's back then than now. Why people with peas, corn, beans, squash would give you some food to cook back then you did not have to pay them for it. People had plenty theay would give you something to eate back in them days. But thing's and people have change farmers of today call that a hand out. People don't want to work. Giving people something to eate has nothing to do with work.

You know the farmer's of today have made so much money of the poor and needy that theay have forgot about God. But just wanted to tell you about the farmers of yester years. Theay feared God. But you know the farmer's of today theay disrespect God. I say because that's what it look like to me. Because when it is raining theay just keep on watering just like its not raining. And when theay don't get any rain, theay stand around an ride around with thaire mouth stuck out. Rember you did not think him for this other rain he gave you.

I can rember when I was about nine or ten years old, when my dad got his land ready to plant cotton, peanuts, and corn. My dad would run the thing that put out the fertilizer. And my mother would run the planter it was the thing that put the seeds in the ground. And a mule pulled each one of them.

Just think a women plowing a mule you know we as poor black people have came a long ways and the struggles is far from being over in 2014. You know as sit here writing these lines I know the struggler is ongoing.

You know where I grew up Ashburn is the only town that I know of that the railroad devide the town. East about 97 percent white west about 99 percent black on the west side of the railroad. You know I don't know how Ashburn got like that, but is so it is what it is. But I don't see Ashburn getting any better but I hope it will but I think we will have to have some more funerals before you see a change in Ashburn. Because weather you know it or not we have people's right here in Ashburn thars glad to see Ashburn the way it is. Theay don't want to see anything to come here. If theay could theay would ??

The Walmart store. That's coming here. You see I was born and raised here. You cannot fool me because I know the people that live here. I know some people that live here that do not know me but trust me I know them. But I know people that know people. So if I want to know something about someone in Ashburn, I will know it and it will be the truth like a guy told me. I can know everything about you in three days. I said you cannot. But guss what he did.

I wonder what Ashburn will be like fifty years from now? I would be afread to say because what I can see is our kid's don't have any jobs. The few jobs out thaire the whites are Mexican have them and the white farmers of today want hire any black's because theay say the young black's want work that's the biggest lie was ever told. Theay will work the farmers just don't want to pay them for working. If you want some one to work you have to pay them a decent salary because theay be thaire grocery from the same store that you by yours. So you know how much your grocery cost. Theay have to pay the same thing too so Ashburn not going anywhere because the people that's here now its training thair children to be just like theay are now.

But you know nobody know how the black race will be it will be a new day with them. But I am not going to get in the future because nobody know's what it holds but God I can say this I hope it will be better than it is now. Ashburn could be made a nice small town next to Interstate 75. But at this time you have so many things in the way. When you have a lot of objects in the way some time you have to wait and let God get involved and move some of that no good stuff out of the way.

You see I did not all about this God stuff. When I was young I was too busy doing the wrong thing. But you know when you done got old like I am you learn to be thankful for how God has brought you in life and he good be ha been to you. You know some people don't beleave in God look what the south did not all of it. But the State of Georgia voted a stupted gun law. Where you can take a gun to clubs, courthouses, churches, schools. WE are all have had a kid's and grownups kill in schools. Weare still haveing people getting killed in clubs.

Well after we got settle in and I sarted to school, I begain to meet some or all the family's that were thair when we got thaire. Thease are some of theam. The Westbrook's these are Remona W. Greens people the Kimble's are people the Burk's, James Burk's people, the Jackson's who are Curtis Pete Jackson people. The Whitsetts who are Tom Whittsetts people. Those are just a few but anyway after I got thaire and met those people and we have been friend's most of us our partant are gone on but we are still here and still friend's.

You know the Bateman family. I been knowing them just as long too. Do anybody know Tommie C. Bateman? I heard of him but never met him. Theay say he is a nice guy. But growing up in Ashburn was better back then than now. We could walk the streets, back then without the police stopping you wanting to know where you are going. What is you got in your pocket? It was just none of that.

We had a little club not far from the project we call the White Ace. I bet some of the guys have forgot the name. WE would go down thaire and play the juke box after school and meet the girls and play around. But you know I can't rember the police ever coming thaire. The girl that ran the place was name Retha. When she left here I never seen her again after she got out of school I don't know what became of her.

WE had a ashouse on the corner from Mr. Bill's store. School teacher Jothon Bennett built that store. Back then theay said he could not sell beer and teach school, but he had grocery to across the road the road. Mr. Preston Dryen had a grocery store. He sold beer and he was a police so way back then. We all know what it was then and still is.

We had a movie theather but some strange reason it burn down. Theay were showing a good movie and all us blacks could not get upstairs. So he let the blacks go down stairs with the whites that night it burned down to the ground. That's why Ashburn don't have a movie.

You think that's bad. I can rember when we black people could not park on Main Street back then. Theay called it the front street. Black's had to park down where Brown's Seafood and French Market and where Fred's are. Back thean people would be on the streets like bees on a honecomb. Mosley white people theay would not move if you where black you would have to walk where the cars were park because the white people would not and let you by.

Back then theay was bad about calling you boy and uncle and preacher. My dad told a man one time he was not a preacher. And told him his name and told him if he could not call him by his name don't call him at all. You know we had some mean black men back then and my dad was one he was not afread of nobody.

Well hello. I want to talk a little more about moonshine. I wonder is anybody in Ashburn know the recipe for moonshine? Yes, I do. I would like to see someone with a moonshine still in some of these woods in Ashburn today. I bet before you could get it sit up the law would know about it.

You know why? Because the people in this town talk too much. You know when my dad and Smith did most of the whiskey running, Johnnie hope some time. But most time he would be in Florida doing other things. One thing about that kind of business you cannot talk to anyone about this kind of business because you don't know who you are talking to. People would talk to my mother about this moonshine and say Arlean this is some good moonshine. Jetty must have ran this himself. Mother smile and said I don't know. I don't have anything to do with that moonshine deal.

Mother would tell me where the matches was when I had to go down and start the fire. My mother would buy me nice cloths to ware to school.

I was one of the well dressed kid in my class. I would see the other kid's talking about everything but would not talk about thair family business. I would never say anything about my family's business. People would ask me. Don't' your daddy run moonshine? I would say I don't know. You have to ask him. But the kids back than was taught back then that what happen at the house, stayed at the house. And do not tell anybody anything.

I am just sitting here thinking a friend of mine live here in Ashburn like I do but he drive a simi big rig. He goes all over the country. So we were sitting down talking and he said yes I new Mr. Jetty when I as a little boy. I use to go with my dad to his house back then when my dad would go up thair I thought he as getting water in those jug's. Later on when I was older he told me what it was moonshine. I ask him did his dad tell him anything else. He said no.

I told him man my dad and three white guys owned a moonshine still back then. And he ask me did I know how to make it? I said yes. And he said Mr. Cleve me and you should sit up one. I told him son the people of today talk too much. The law know it before we got set up. And I told him you don't have white men that own land would do that. I would be afread to even ask one because the only thing he would do is run and tell the law.

I told him always when you are going to do something with someone make sure you know that person and his background. Now the people in those hills and montains in North Georgia are still running moonshine up thaire d you cannot pay a law man to go up in thim hills. Because those people have look out people watching with guns and the law up thaire know that. So I guss theay are afread. I cannot blame them because people watching with guns and the law up thaire know that. So I guss theay are afread. I cannot blame them because people in that kind of business theay are for real. That's thaire livehood and theay are not going to let the law or nobody else mess it up.

I think the lawmen in North Georgia are more smarter than ours in South Georgia because the first thing these down here do is call everybody and theay would get everybody killed up thaire.

You know in 1952 we moved from the country off the farm about 8 miles north of Ashburn from a place call Sibley. Of the William's Place my dad was a share cropper. It was a lot of black familys staying on the place but most of them ewre moeving to. So dad had been down here and seen about a job and the man hired him. Mr. John Raines him and his brother Mr. Marvin Raines ran a sawmill. So dad came back and told us to start packing so we did. I was 14 years old at that time so I was glad to move to town Ashburn. Little did I know Ashburn would be like it is now. But we moved to the housing project thaire we stayed for 11 years and guss what when we moved our rent was only $11.00 a month.

I can't remember what it was when we first moved in but man that was a pretty place. The lawn's was pretty and green you could not even see the ground. And theay had signs saying keep off the grass. You could not park in the drive way between the apartments. It was for emergency fire truck and E.M.T.'s you park in. It you were in trouble if you got caught but those apartments on the inside was beautiful. You know what theay heated with Kerosene and it did not take much to heat the apartment with because theay were new so we had a good place to stay and I love thair.

I am sitting down on this beautiful Sunday morning read in a history book. I was look at a picture of an old black man plowing a mule in the deep South and I thought about how my dad did the same thing when he was sharecropping walk a hundred miles a day behind a plow just for the young people who read this book. A plow is something a mule pull to tiller the earth where you can plant the seed's on the farm. Ok. My pore dad work from sun up to sundown. And lesten at the end of the year his boss would say Jetty your cleared seven hundred dollars this year.

But look at all the work that he done for those seven hundred dollars. You know that kind of money back was a lot of money for a black man to have in the south. But back then seven hundred dollars was like two or three thousand you could get something for your money. But now days the stores are robbers the peoples theay are selling some stuff in the stores for three prices. Our government need to step in and make them regelate the prices. This is happen in 2014 our people will always be poor. If our government don't make the store's releglate thair prices because it is a shame how you do up town to the grocery store and spend one hundred dollars. And come out of the store with two plastic bags of grocery. When you have one grocery store that's what you get. I wish we could get more grocery stores in West Ashburn and clothing stores over thaire.

I was born in this country. In a small town about 200 miles south of Atlanta, Georgia with about 9000 people city and county. I was raised up here. Now I am a senior. As a black race of people we have been labled. All our life we have been called negro and blacks, afro American. That's fine but to go around saying we want work is an insult to the black race.

Why? Because it is a lie and I get tird of lesten at people say it. Because our ancestor helped build this country with thair sweat and blood.

But thaire is a God who sits high and look low and he knows the heart of every man. I been to alot of places and the only place I have heard that the young black's want work is here in Ashburn. We have a lot of young black's working in other places like Albany, Tifton, Cordele, and Sylvester. I would not call these fast food places no job for a fiamley man. People love to bet on the Mexicans. Yes theay will work and some of them and some whites want work ether. But are never talk about. I agree some of my people are lazy.

But I can never here anything about that on the street. So what is everybody going to do when all those hard working illegals be pick up by ICE. Its going to happen because we have more illegals than we do legal because I now all of the Mexicans. I seen here in the Turner County was not born in the U.S.A.

I know one black man told me he ask a man at the store about a job and he said the man told him y'all want work. He said he did not know what to say. You know what I said mean if he don't want you to work I don't know what to tell you?

But that's what happen when we are lied on you notice I said we because I am a black man myself before I retired I was in the work force. I did never here anything about black's young or older. Would not work. You see when I was working we did not have all of these Mexican illegals and legals because back then where I work theay would not hire them because theay new theay was illegals.

But people don't care anymore. Theay will take a chance for chepe labor. It's not my people want work but when theay work, theay want to get paid a recent salrley. In these young black's have never work on a farm. Theay don't know anything about picking produce. Thaire parant are factory workers. Theay kid's don't know anything about farm work. I know that we be labeled. I know someone out thaire going to call me a racist but I am not. Are you? I am just telling the truth.

So if everybody out thaire would tell the truth we would get along better. You know you can fool the people sometime but not all the time. See we as a race of people understand on another. But do y'all understsand us?

My brothers and sisters lets stop being blind to the problems that are destroying our black and white brothers and sisters today. Along with drugs, crack cocaine, and powder cocaine, heroin, and more you get a whole lot more thein just a high. Mans strong desires, ambitions and wills to destroy mankind with many different forms of diseases. I would like to send a message to those that are not aware our just plain don't care. As the sun rise each morning to govern the days. So rise man to condem the mind's and bodies of others.

As we observe on a day today basis that the world is being plagued by aid's and its carrier. Crake cocaine and its users turns to hatred. Violence and sometime murder of each other peoples its time to wake up and take full control of our lives and stop being misled by others. Its time to render ourselves to God who is our Savior and redeemer. The only one who has the power to give us strength that we don't have. But so desperately need in order to clear up our very confused people's.

I would just like to say to you a lot of people wish theay never was fool to try it. Just like smokeing and dranking I use to drank real bad. Nobody could tell me anything about drankng. I was always saying I know what I am doing.

Did I know anything? My dad tried to talk to me I would tell him I am a grown man. He said ok. I will treat you like you are a grown man. About two left hooks later and one right cross I had second thought about who I was. But he knock some sense in my big head. And he is gone on. But I will never forget that day and I think him it hope me.

I know a lot of people on both sides of town that use drug's. But putting them in jail is not helping them. The jail is not a doctor. We know what theay need so let's help them. Theay are God's people like we are. If we walk around talk about and not try to help them we are just as bad as theay are in God's eye sight because theay can't help themselves, but we can.

You know as a person who helped make moonshine I can tell you a lot about it. For one thing it will make you drunk. I have often thought about whiskey. Now you can have moonshine in a bottle sit it on the table it will sit thaire six month's. If nobody pick it up it will stay right thaire. But when you pick it up. If you just pour you a small shot and drank it, you will be ok.

But some people is not going to do that. Because when I was dranking I did not. I am not a shame to tell it. I had to quit dranking because I had got where I did not know how to drank. I would turn up a bottle and would not take it down until it was empty. I was nothing but a drunk. I quit dranking in 1983. And man all my people was glad my dad was more glad theian anybody because I was the bookkeeper for his businesses he ran a logging, pulpwood, medical transport. I did all of the book work. I did all of the other stuff.

But when I was dranking I would take care all of the time figuring the time and do the paying off before I take a drank. I would just only drank on weekends. My dad was so glad when I quit he did not know what to do he told me. Boy I can put all my trust in you now. He said think you Jesus you answer my prayer. I can trust him to handle all my business now. Don't get it wrong. My dad trusted me to handle his business but alot of times we would have to go and look at timber.

This is Ashburn where I grew up. I don't care how much education you have you want never be number in anything. I look at our school's staff. It has never had a black football or basketball head coach. It always has to be assistant coach. Why do we as a black race of people in small town's in the deep south have to be second on everything? We are tax payers just like Mr. John so why can't we be respected like everybody was working togeather.

I never heard the word about young blacks want work. But I here it here. But no where elses I wonder why. I would sure like to know who got that started. Theay, I mean the farmers of Turner County, you don't see any black's on the farm or on the tractor's anymore because the tractors of today is just lack a car theay are cabin theay have A.C. radio C.D. Players and all theat good stuff. So you no longer have a need for blacks on the farm unless theay are picking your produce and theay don't do that.

You all say theay want work. Well tell me who drove y'all tractors when theay was not cabin the (Mexicans) or black's. I think back I the fifty's when them black men would be on them tractors and it would so cold. But do theay get thinked, no thair grandkids get lable as the people want work but thair grand partant worked for nothing.

Weekends. My dad and I ran moonshine trunk enough but that as behind us and when he was buying timber he did not want the people to smell whiskey on me. Now that's the kind of man my dad was. He was all about business and that's the way it supose to be. I will tell anybody thait don't drank. Don't start. I know I have helped to make it and I also dranked it so nobody out thair can tell me about dranking or maken it.

It is funny if you drink on glass of moonshine that glass full will take over your whole body when you are high you can't walk strate. Your legs are wobbly. You slure in your talk. It just take control of the whole body you reflex are not as quick. Your vision are not good eather.

To sum it all up, you are not the same persion. Any time you get high off any thing it changes you all the way round. Trust me I knew Trust me I know about whiskey. I have never did drugs of any kind. No more theain pain pills when I get sick and even then I try to get around take them then. I don't think its anyone in Ashburn or Turner county that know as much about moonshine as I do. I know a couple of guys but I am quite sure thaire is more than we think it was a lot of land an stuff bought in Turner County and a lot bought with drug money and still being bought.

But here in Ashburn where I grew up, it is against the law for us to do anything but work. You know I asked black police offer, I said if the citizens can ride around and see drugs being sold, I am quite sure you guys can. You know what he told me? He said we was told some things you have to turn your head to. That's something for the law to tell a citizen.

Today is July 1, 2014. My cousin Machal Mathis brought honor to Ashburn an Turner county and the State of Georgia by being placed 7th in the nation in keyboarding application in Washington, D.C. during the FGLA national Leadership conference which was held the week of July 7 -11. Michael is the son of Nell and Carroll Mathis.

After winning region competition In Albany earlier in the year, Michael competed in the State competition in Atlanta, Georgia where he brought home top honors by becoming the first black Turner County Fbla member to win the state championship inside the Washington convetion center where the presidential inaugural ball is held and among thousands of spectators and hundreds of supporters waving flags and Georgia banners.

Michael was awarded an FBLA plaque as he was ranked #7 in the nation in keyboarding applications. The family of Machael Mathis thanks everyone who helped to make his trip to Washington, D.C. a success. Turner County High School administration staff, superintendent Jimmy Alberson, Ashburn women's club, Community National Bank, National Bank, D.C. and Mrs. J.C. Green, Ashburn Bank, Mr. and Mrs. John Dye, Jr. and Mrs. Hodge King, Ashburn Rotary Club, Mr. and Mrs. John Y. Cristian, Mr. and Mrs. Rex Giddens, Dr. and Mrs. E.J. Tifon, Feltine Cross, Mr. and Mrs. John E. Paulk, III, Ms. Jessie Muse of Mitchellville, M.D., Jessie Payne, Jr. of Charlotte, N.C., Mr. and Mrs. Jessee Payne, Mr. and Mr. W.J. Bell, Mrs. Wilathrel Rodgers and New Harvest Church of Christ, and all of Montegomery Albama. I wonter why I see none of this at the school he attended none whatsoever. Not even in the library. Out of all the white support he had still did not get any from the City or

Mayor of Ashburn. Back then you were lucky to get a hand shake.

I can't help from feeling the way I do about where I grew up. You see we had three guys that was raised here in Ashburn that went pro. What I mean about that is playing professional football. Theay went to school here. You never here anyone say anything about those guys. Some of the kids going to school today probley don't know that Big Ben Thomas, the Crockett Brothers, and Big Sanders and Ben are cousin. But you see the people in Asbhurn this theay names are never mention. I wonder would any one talk about or name something after them if theay were white.

This is what I have a problem with. Small towns like Ashburn do and the other small towns in the deep south. So the same games as played in the pass are slowly trying to crepe back in, but we are not going to play the same game twice. Game is out.

I was talking with a friend of mine the other day. I told him, man what thank about all of these people coming to this country? He said Cleve man I don't know it is making it hard for us and we were born here. Our country is letting all of these illegal people from other countrys come here. I know. If I was the president I would put traps to the bordor. The President know how to stop it. Put troops at the border. The Republicans then would say know. You are going to kill woman and children. You see understand. The problem the president have with a Republican congress. I don't think most American do had theay did theay would not be blaming the president. The president is not to blame.

Where I grew up, you know we had our first black police chief around the year of 1988. Nobody did not. Everybody was surprised that Ashburn had Chief Davis. We were proud of him, but little did we know that the mayor at that time had a plan for the chief and the plan was to control the police chief.

And it begain I don't think the new chief caught on until the black's started to talking. You could go up thaire and ask the chief to do something for you he would say I'm sorry my hand's are tied. He was the chief by name, but at that time the mayor was chief of police and mayor, Chief James Davis was just wareing the badge but you have heard that all good things come to an end.

James finely figured out what was going on. James made a u turn and got his self togeathur. So, he call a meeting one night. He wanted to talk with all black mail's. All of us older guy's went to the meeting because we wanted to see what the chief had to say. So the chief got up and told all of the young men, he said you guys got to do better because I am tired of putting you guys in jail. That night I told this other man that was sitting next to me, I said to the guy somebody in here is going to call the mayor tonight. And he said you are kidding. I said watch and see. And sure enough the next week the mayor and chief had some word's. Something about a chair the mayor said the chief did not get puchers's order to get the chair with or some kind of crap.

It's 2014 and I work over at the splash pad. Better known Southwest Georgia as a water park, and we have staff manger's who are all black. Myself and three more I don't know why white's did not apply this year. Theay had one last year he got fired because the rules he was suppose to enforce he was breaking them. I notice sense I have been working thaire the white people don't want a black person to tell them what to do.

I know this I been throught it. When you try to explane the rules to them, theay want to ask a lot of quiston's when all theay have to do is take a little time and read the rule's at the gate. But you know theay still think the rules don't apply to them and that's sad because rule's are not colored. Theay are for everyone. The bad part is theay are bringing thaire kids up that way. This age in time here where I grew up. I have been saying Ashburn an Turner County was doing good. But I have some doubt sense I been working at the water park.

And these are not old people. Some are young and middle age people. I feel sorry for them because theay are acting like kids. But I guss that is the way theay were program. But I can tell just as soon as out of town white's walk in the gate's theay are not from Ashburn or Southwest Georgia. Why? Because theay speake to you with a smile. And don't walk in the gates acting like theay are mad with the world.

What is wrong with the white people in the deep south? Why do theay say theay don't hate us blacks? But treat us like a disease. What theay need to understand is it will never be like it was in the 50's and 60's. Those days are gone and want be back. Don't look for them.

I be around a lot of white people on the job and off the job and you can see the way theay do and say things that theay wish it was back in the 50's and 60's. Because that's what is wrong with them. Theay do not want poor people to make any money especially black's. That's what all this hate is about. It is still some good white people here but theay are afread to say anything when black's are mistreated. Because theay have told me, that's wrong but I can't say anything. To me if it's wrong say something. But theay want and that is what keeps small town's in the south devided.

So don't forget racism in Ashburn is a long way from being gone especailly with the older people. Theay try to hide it but cannot because all black's can pick up on it real quick. Some white's try to hide it. I can pick up on it quick. Some white's try to hide it. I can pick up on it quick. I have work for people that was racist. Guss theay thought theay had me fooled, but guss what. It was funny to me because theay thought theay had me fooled but I knew it. So what it is white people know that we are smarter than theay are that is why theay try to keep money out our hands by trying to work us chepe and don't want our kid to get a good education. You see every time that you try to do something to a black person, it is not a surprise we be looking for it. You might keep money out our had's for now, but one day you will woke up and you will be working for us or one of our brother's of color.

Back then on Steven Street and all around that naborhood was a good place to live. I know I will have some people to say that was long ago. You are right. It was so we should be better now that we was and we wrent bad. But you see when I came along everybody hope rase everybody's children. See if I went down to Mrs. Mary's house to play with her kid's and did wrong and Mrs. Mary whip my butt. If I did not want to get another whipping, don't tell my mother.

You see mother's back then are not like mother's today. Whip me she would say what was you doing. Now you know we are going to lie and say nothing back then that was the wrong thing to say. Mothers back then would say no-no-no-no you are lying Mrs. Mary would not whip you for nothing. But I am going to beat your butt and you will know how to play the next time you go down thaire.

But mothers of today. I know because I have some kinfolk that are young mothers. Theay come around and be talking girl I wish that bitch would hit my child. You should have came along when I did. Those mothers would whip your child and you too we had some mothers back then I know I got butt whipping from my grandmothers Aunt's then I did my mother and I rember all of them theay made a beller man out of me. I might go tomorrow but I never beent to prison or got in any serious trouble like I said I might go but I hope not.

Can any one rember what Dr. King said about his dream. What did he say about little black boy's and little white girls will be playing togeather. We see that today and we are going to see more than that. We might not see it too much in Ashburn. But change is comeing so we might as well get ready.

What people need to do is not try to live in the past live for now. If you don't want to change, don't do thing's to try and stop peopley's that want change. I use to here my grandmother say if you are not going don't hender me. That's what I say if you want to live in the 50's.

In 2014, don't try to recruit people who want change to stay back with you. You know I hate to brag but we have some of the smartis black's in the world. Look at our president he is a smart and strong man. If he had not ben theay, the Republicans would have been got him out of the white house. Theay told the country when he was elected in 2008 that theay was not going to help him do anything and hope he fall and about a year or two back congress said theay did not want a black man telling them what to do.

Old as I am, I can't rember any congress saying that about any president. I just want to tell this country that we live in that we have a racis congress. I have never been people before that hate people's because the color thair skin but you know what, God is watching the people that or supose to be helping lead this country but are blocking the president.

I wonder why people will relize that it is 2014 and not 1914 and start acting like it is. You know when I was raised up here in Ashburn, my parent taught me to speak to everybody. No matter what olor theay was. So you see if you have people that hate us blacks that much down in the south, no wonder our kid's are failing grade's in school. I hat to say it like this, but it is what it is. You know theay already call us the dirty south and look like some part of the south is trying to live up to that name and that's not good.

You know some time I run into people that try to use word that was use in slavery like boy and Hay that is not good. I never seen a boy in his 70's have you. I call that disrespect don't you? I would never address a grown man as a boy. Would you? I would say sir. If I did not know his name, but you know that we as a black race of people has alway's been named as a nobody. But I just want everybody to know that we are somebody. I will never except us as a nobody.

So people you can trash that nobody its dead and want be back. I have always watch people the way theay act. The way theay talk. And you can tell if theay are racis or not but you know. If you work around white people enough or do business with them, it will show up no matter how theay try to hide it. It will show up. Some will say theay are not. You know why because theay can't see it and we can. Know you cannot blame them because that's the way theay were taught. But you can blame them as grown people for not learner better.

Moonshine and Living in the Deep South

I know Ashburn is a small town everybody know everybody. I been around white people all my life, but I got common sense to know that theay don't love us blacks. But theay play a good role. But some of them will let you know up front. Most all of us black's here in Ashburn know that we have klan members here in Ashburn and the good part is we know who theay are. But as long as theay don't mess with us we are ok with it. A person has a right to be a member of anything theay want to.

You know we black's in Ashburn we older one's have to keep the young black's in line like our police officer be hairassing our young men. If it was not for us older mens like myself, it would be hell here a lot of time's. White people don't understant. To be black and been through what we have is hell. And our ancestors went through was worst than what we are going through.

But you now some white's will say I don't see anything wrong. No, you don't want to see what your ancestors created. But its thaire. I will name just a few things that is holding us back underpaid. Want give us the good jobs change the way we hire. I don't care what kind of education we have you want to start us off with $7.25 per hour, but if you are white start off pay is around nine dollars or more. These are some of the things we have had to put up with in the south for the last two or three hundred years. I wonder could white people's could have made it like we did.

I wonder do we have any white family's in Ashburn that would do like I seen a family do on TV. Theay decided theay would try to live off what we are being payed minimum wages. I think theay did it for some month's I can't rember how many but when theay got through and came back on TV, theay said theay don't see how anyone can make it on minimum wage. Theay said a couple with two kid's cannot make it. But most whites today do not want to pay you anything to work buy $7.25 per hour and when you want work for that, theay will say you want work but theay want tell why.

That is why a lot of your large company's come down south because theay can get the people in the south to work chepe. And theay love Georgia because Georgia is a at will state and theay can pretty much do the way theay want to do with labor. Because theay think the people down south and don't know anything about the unions. And some of them are we as a black race of people have never been treated right in the southern states and the deeper you get down in south Georgia the worst it get.

I know a white lady that move to Ashburn from up North. She told me she use to read about down here but did not beleave it until she move here. She said she could not beleave wat she seen and heard she quit one job at a gas station because she got tird of those old white men's talking about black people and using the N word. She told her boss she could not take that anymore. Because where she came from the people don't do that.

You know I work at the water park here in town Ashburn and I get a chance to talk to a lot of people. I also talk to a lot of people from other county's who has never seen a splash pad. You know when you talk with a lot of woman, theay are going to talk about everything. I was talking to a lady one day about school and how our black kid's are failing in school. I did not know she as a teacher. And she said Mr. Brown our kids are failing because the white teacher do not know how to reach black kid's or don't want to teach them.

I replyed and said you know I was not for desergated school in the first place and millions of black's felt just like I did. Because when you force something on two races of people, this is what you get one race is going to get short changed. But you know it was our government. I though back then that Dr. King and the civil rights movement was wrong back then and I still do. Look how our black kid's are failing in the school's not only in Ashburn. It's in all school's that was forced to mix. But I guss Dr. King thought back then it was time for a change.

But the people did not want change back then and I did not know you felt like that. I said I do. You see the black kid's are the one's who are suffering behind this. Don't get me wrong, Dr. King did some good things for this country. Try but desergation of schools I think was a bad choce.

Dr. King done alot for us as a blacks. I came up in the days of segregation. I know how we had to go to back doors, back café windows. Ride in the back seat of buses. All of this was good. But to force school's to mix is not working like Dr. King was intent for it to work.

I know you? We know that we had people back thean that did not like us blacks and we have people today that do not like us. I think it is not right for our kids to not get a good education because of something theay don't know anything about. I heard this more times and little.

That white teacher's cannot teach black kids because theay don't know how. Our kid's are not like white kid's and that's where the problem is. You see some of our kids and that's where the problem is. You see some of our kids learn faster than the other's and some do not.

I know you heard this one. All of y'alls is just alike. But we are not so I think that is the problem in school with the white teachers. Theay don't know how and theay just pass them to the next grade without them knowing the grade theay was in. But most of the time in these school's you have a white principal and he is not going to do anything to a white teacher down here in the south. So this is the way theay let you know theay don't like mix school's. Don't get me wrong. Thair are some white people that don't like what goes on in our school's. Here in Ashburn and all other school's But are afread to say anything. But that is some of the reason why our children's are falling behind and don't seem like anybody care.

I beleave every person should have a right to go anywhere theay want to. And be with anyone theay want to be with. But in the South you can do this but somewhere down the road you will pay. Getting a job or getting a pay raise. You down here where I grew up is like that. But older people's like myself can see things our young people can't see like our young black brothers cannot see. If I was going to do anything, I would be for me.

We have a lot of young black men in prison down here and right here for selling drug's for other people. The white man but who go to prison the black man. I can tell you it was not like that back in the day when my dad, Smith, and Ralph, who were white but not like the whites of today. Those guys were real true white men's not fake white men's of today. But yes the south is some better because theay don't punch black's down here anymore. And go to black's home and drag them out and beat them up. So you see it's got some better. But you can cross your finger. You know it is still some people wish it was like that now.

I don't wish that. Because blood would be running down the ditche's like water. Because we blacks has already said it will be no more like it was in this lifetime. Never. We are all in this world togeather or we can die togeather because we as a black race of people are not going anywhere. God put us on his earth togeather. No man owns nothing.

You know I read the paper some time. People are saying we going to take our country back. You don't own anything. This is God's world.

I was talking with some people about affirmative of action. Theay were some friends of mine and theay said we need it. I said yes we do. But is not working. You see we had it back in 1960 and it was not working and it is not working now. Why I say it is not working where I grew. And nowhere in the South.

I done some research and found out how much each race of people were making in the year of 2000. It did not give me a name of the town or state but for the amout of money was being made it has to be a southern state. The median weekly earning for blacks was $459.00, for Latinos $395.00 weekly. For white's $590.00 weekly. You can see how uneven the playing field. I don't think the people even worry about obaying the law. And theay wrote it. And still theay found ways an loopholes to get by I our government is not going to do any thing to them because the government is white.

But let one of us black's try to brake the law's and see what happen. That kind of stuff show you how much our government care about the American Blacks. Almost nothing and I am quite sure it is a lot or more black's out thair feel just like it do.

Ok. Not long after that a white man killed another kid in Florida. I think when our government seen that the state as not going to do anything theay should have step in and took care business and then maybe the other kid that got shot would proble be living because the white guy would have not killed the other kid because he would have been afread. But our government did not do nothing.

www.ingramcontent.com/pod-product-compliance
Lightning Source LLC
Chambersburg PA
CBHW071519080526
44588CB00011B/1481